PAUL JENNINGS

Paul Jennings is one of Britain's most popular and prolific humorous writers. A former columnist with *The Observer*, he has been appreciated by all who love good humour through his contributions to *Punch*, for which he has been writing since the end of the war, and his many bestselling books, including *Oddly Enough, I Was Joking Of Course* and *The Jenguin Pennings*. His hobbies are madrigal singing and thinking about writing a vast, serious book.

PUN FUN

compiled by Paul Jennings

Hamlyn Paperbacks

PUN FUN

ISBN 0 600 20001 9

First published in Great Britain 1980
by Hamlyn Paperbacks
Copyright © 1980 by Paul Jennings
and M. K. K. Brown

Hamlyn Paperbacks are published by
The Hamlyn Publishing Group Ltd,
Astronaut House, Feltham,
Middlesex, England
(Paperback Division: Hamlyn Paperbacks,
Banda House, Cambridge Grove,
Hammersmith, London 6W oLE)

Set, printed and bound in Great Britain by
Cox & Wyman Ltd, Reading

CONTENTS

INTRODUCTION

Ideally this book should not be read. It should be broadcast. Unlike children, puns should be heard, not seen. (I say, that's just come to me. This isn't going to be as hard as I thought.) Puns are made by people in convivial company, aware of the quicksilver nature of language, people not afraid to laugh at their own jokes because they know they are in the company of others who have this true, profound instinct that the world is not what we think it is, being full of surprise, having another side; people, in other words, with a sense of humour.

It was on radio that the pun, that supreme verbal example of the rug being pulled from under you, reached its greatest heights. And splendid though it is to see on the printed page such a dialogue as this:

'I wonder why the Germans are holding their fire?'
'Perhaps they haven't got a fireplace.'

it helps to know that it took place between Ned Seagoon and Eccles. The programme *I'm Sorry, I'll Read That Again*, of happy memory, was a long succession of mostly terrible puns, relished by an appreciative audience of Groaners Class A. (I'll explain what these and Class B are in a moment.) 'We'd only been in the jungle a week when our food ran out.' *Clop clop clop effects.* 'Come back, food!' 'Well, there's only one thing to do, ring up the curtain.' *Brrr-brrr, brrr-brrr.* 'Hello, curtain speaking.' 'That was a curtain call . . .'

It's an old radio tradition, going back to *Take it From Here* (Jimmy Edwards, dying at end of cod film epic about moustachioed Mexican rebel: 'Well, I've only one thing to say.

Hacienda.' '*Hacienda?*' 'Yes, *hacienda* the film'), and the father of them all, *ITMA*.

I've probably said enough already to make sure that Groaners Class B put this book down in disgust and move on to another book, such as *Roadside Tree of Malaya*, or *The Sociology of Sex*, or something. Groaners Class A are wryly aware that there is a tradition of groaning at puns (established, I'm inclined to think, by Groaners Class B, who are either envious at not having thought of it themselves or, worse still, really do actually hate puns and the whole life-loving respect for the endless humour-resources latent in language). They will groan, for instance, at many of the puns in this book, as they are meant to (e.g. aspersion – a donkey from Iran; Vienna is the city of Strauss and strain; etc.). But they will groan in a friendly way and whenever they hear an elegant one they will lapse into awed silence.

I'm not going to come out on a limb and give an example of an elegant one from this book, although there are plenty of them, as well as terrible ones. For the fact is that elegant delivery can make a terrible pun sound brilliant, and vice versa. I mean, there's one in this book that doesn't look so good on the page: 'What has four legs and a trunk?' 'That's irrelevant!' 'That's-a-right, irrelevant!' But sanctified for all time among us paranomasiamaniacs as an exchange between Chico and Groucho Marx . . .

Paronomasia, as many punnologists know (and you needn't think I coined that word, it's in the *Oxford English Dictionary*), is merely the classical name for punning. There is probably a time and a place for presenting the case for the pun in a serious philosophical way, but this is not it. I will merely point out that many real philosophers have done so, e.g. of course Bergson, who thought it arose from regarding words as *things,* counters, mere dead sounds, almost objects, without regard for their true, spiritual meaning. 'The absent-mindedness of language', he said.

Come to think of it, the ultimate pun *is* perhaps visual. Dr

Spooner (like many theologians, attempting to name the Un-nameable, tripping over words: 'You have tasted a whole worm', etc.) knew vaguely that the best you can do if you spill claret on a white tablecloth is to put some salt on it and hope no one will notice. But only he would have spilt salt and then poured claret on the little heap.

The puns in this book are neither visual nor aural. Just printed. This is a cross between a reference book and a compost heap, if you can imagine such a thing (and punnologists can imagine *anything*). You will probably have noticed that it isn't limited to puns as such, relying on the two meanings or sounds of the same word.

There are all sorts of kindred word-jokes: misprints, mal-apropisms, definitions ('pedagogue, one who gets excited about feet'), and whatever classification this one comes under: 'Please excuse ym shguoc dna sezeens, but I've got this terrible code.'

It includes those complicated stories that enable the teller, if there is anyone left to listen, to end with some such line as 'Oh, my baking yak!' or 'To air is human, but to forklift divine,' and of course the one that ends 'All your Basques in one exit'. That's the point about the compost heap. You can put practically any-thing in it.

There are even bits of verse, and pieces of sustained creative fantasy like the place-name sequence on pages 29–30, for my vast team of researchers has reported that when you go out into the pun world it begins to take over. Known in the trade as 'hamlynguists', their presence always betrayed by manic laughter, they soon come to believe their own fantasies, such as the historical reason why Browning mentions them in *The Pied Piper of Hamelin*. Oh yes, he does:

You should have heard the Hamlyn people
Ringing the bells till they rocked the steeple.

What have bells got to do with puns, you might ask, and even if you don't I shall explain. In the early, primitive days of pun

9

research, before the railway system was properly developed, pun researchers going out on field trips had to take their own equipment, for they often ventured into wild country where, let alone grammar or sense, there weren't even any hotels, and they had to take tents, field rations, canvas chairs, and so on. They thus came to be known as camp punnologists. Take it or leave it.

This was long before the word *camp* had acquired its present connotation. Hamlynguists are at home not only in the pub or the street, but also in the high world of literature from Shakespeare and before to James Joyce and after, full of great lusty unashamed puns.

The treasures and dross brought together here should remind us of two solemn truths. One is that one man's treasure is another man's dross. The other is that some puns approximate to the Pure Form of the pun, they are already *there*, a kind of Platonic ideal, simply waiting for some human mind to tune in to them.

Thus. About ten years ago, when I was lighting the first fire of the autumn with some rather damp wood, various woodlice, spiders, and other insects began scurrying frantically about, usually towards the hottest or smokiest part, stupid fools. I had a touch of conscience and thought I should perhaps save them from death by fire. 'They must wonder what the hell has happened,' I said to my wife. 'All the summer in this nice peaceful log, then suddenly all this smoke and flame. They must think it's the end of the world.'

'Yes,' she said, confirming yet again how right I was to marry her, 'I expect they're saying, "Armageddon out of here." '

When we were married our best man was, and for that matter still is, what used to be known as an incorrigible punster. Our friendship survived the acid test of a shared villa holiday in France with young children of both families. One day our two wives were making the kind of vast communal omelette which is the staple dish in such circumstances. They had got up to eighteen eggs when he said, 'I say, don't you think an *oeuf* is an *oeuf*?'

This is a good example of a bilingual pun, and brings me to the only example I know of a pun translated. It is slightly different in the two languages, but never mind. English: 'What is life? It depends on the liver.' In French: *'Qu'est-ce que c'est que la vie? C'est matière de foi.'* *Foi* (faith) or *foie* (liver). Rich, eh?

Once, my father-in-law, who was among other things the editor of *Grove's Dictionary of Music* and a great scholar, was laughing so much *in his sleep* that it woke him up. It seems he had a dream in which he was handing round drinks to a lot of young married women with the words 'a port in every wife'.

Once – no, I must stop and let you browse. If you are a punnologist (and what are you *doing* with this book if you aren't?) it is just the thing for a browse. It's another question whether high browse or low browse will . . . aaaargh!

I

PUNNY MONEY

Puns crop up everywhere, in formal speech, everyday speech, books, newspapers, on the radio, the television, and at the cinema. I saw an advertisement on television recently which claimed:

The prices are all-inclusive. There are no hidden extras, like this and VAT.

Other 'taxes' which cry out for punning are syntax and surtax.

Syntax is what the girls at the local brothel pay to the police.

And:

Surtax is a kind of knight duty.

The following type of pun – and there are lots of similar ones throughout this book – is called a Tom Swiftie (goodness knows why!):

'I've sent my cheque to the wrong charity,' she said with some misgiving.

Two more cheque puns are these:

'Do you accept cheques at this restaurant?'

'Of course, sir, as long as they behave themselves.'

And:

In desperation, the dwarf from Prague pounded on his friend's front door. 'The Russian police are after me!' he cried. 'Won't you please cache a small Czech?'

The pun sterling:

I put all my savings on a horse, and now I'm a saddler but wiser man.

Saving money is one area where nothing succeeds like excess.

The hard part of being broke is watching the rest of the world go buy.

One of the grotesque aspects of seventeenth- and eighteenth-century art is that if you buy too much of it, you end up baroque.

I've put my money into a new girlie magazine so I can take accrued interest.

Trying to make a good impression, the idiot told the heiress that he wanted to marry her for her Monet.

When she said that I could make her mine,
Then I knew she was just a gold-digger.

Capital was her Seoul aim because she was a Korea girl.

A bearded prospector marched into an assayer's office back in the California gold rush days and plonked half a dozen huge nuggets on to the counter. The clerk stood there looking amazed. 'Well,' rasped the forty-niner angrily, 'don't just stand there. Assay something!'

One millionaire used to refer to his long-haired hippie son as the 'hair apparent'.

And then there was the millionaire whose only son was run over one day by a steamroller. His obituary notice referred to him as a 'compressed heir'.

A millionaire was being shown over his son's university by the Vice-Chancellor. Said the millionaire, 'I'm most impressed by the university. Could it use some financial assistance?' Replied the Vice-Chancellor, 'Endow!'

Millionaires are often referred to as the upper crust. Does that make them a lot of crumbs held together by dough, just because they've got the bread?

An old Apache Indian who had become a millionaire when oil was discovered on his tribe's reservation was very pleased when his three sons were finally accepted for membership in a very expensive yachting club. For years, it seems, his one ambition had been to see his red sons in the sail set!

Some people make their money illegally . . .

Only a fool would milk his company of expenses when none has been in curd.

Said the magistrate, 'Now tell me, why did you steal that purse?' Replied the woman in the dock, 'I wasn't feeling too well, your Honour, and I felt the change would do me good!'

A stockbroker in the City illegally borrowed some of his customers' securities. Of course, the 'loan' was only a temporary one, and the stockbroker returned the securities. Indeed, he made the error of returning too many. When he was eventually found, he got a stiff sentence for being generous to a vault.

Some natives stumbled on what they thought was the legendary treasure of the pirate Captain Kidd. The leader was afraid that they would be found out, and that Kidd would have them all arrested at the very least. So the leader decided to hide the loot in his grandfather's apiary. He passed a note to his second-in-command, which read: Booty is in the beehives of the older.

The prisoners' idea of getting together an orchestra failed. Why? Because they all wanted the lute, of course!

Even children can be roped into money puns:
When Alphonse was a baby, his parents hired a nanny just to push him in his pram. Like most other people, he's been pushed for money ever since.

And then there was the sign seen outside the main entrance to a fair:
Children under fourteen must be accompanied by money and daddy.

Inflation, galloping or roaring . . .
Pity the poor man who has a big load of debt and doesn't know how to budge it.

Interest is a crude income.

A-hunting we will go,
A-hunting we will go!
That's the way to get a buck,
Or at least a little doe!

One of Wall Street's financial experts believes that the stock market rises and falls as the length of ladies' skirts rises and falls. Miniskirts and the so-called glamour stocks soared in 1967. Hemlines and conglomerates went down together during 1968. Hot pants came in in 1971 and the stock market on Wall Street rose to new heights. The moral of the financial expert: 'Don't sell until you see the heights of their thighs!'

2

THE PUN IS MIGHTIER THAN THE SWORD

Religious puns can range from old chestnuts like 'the piece of cod which passeth all understanding' and 'gladly, the cross-eyed bear' to more everyday efforts.

A church fair is a bazaar experience . . .

Extreme Protestants are against combining the churches; they want no potpourri.

Priests can't marry without prior approval.

The priest jogged round the graveyard in order to exorcise his spirit.

A Puritan is a man who noes what he likes.

She was a nice girl, but he rector.

'The Mother Superior says that if I don't study harder, I'll be in this convent for reverend ever.'

Is a lay preacher an advocate of free love?

The minister of one particular small church was his own bookkeeper. His bills were neatly filed away in a box marked 'Due Unto Others'.

The rural vicar decided that he would try to raise chickens in order to supplement his income. Each morning, he went out into the garden to see if the eggs he had bought had hatched. Finally, one morning, he found they all had, and there were dozens of fluffy little chicks. 'Ah,' he murmured thankfully, 'my coop runneth over.'

When the bishop was at his barber's one day, he became aware of a rather strange odour. 'What's that strange smell?' he demanded. 'Oh,' said his barber. 'Forgive me, Father, for I have singed.'

Even the Three Wise Men and God Himself are not immune . . .
The Three Wise Men each carried only one gift because they had believed in travelling light.

If you climb on to the top of an active volcano, you can see the creator smoking.

When a New York underground newpaper ran a letter to the editor protesting about the way a reader thought the paper was deifying sex, the letter appeared under the heading 'In God We Thrust'.

Places of worship succumb, too:
The reason the old church in our village has irregular recesses in its walls is that the builder lost the plans. In consequence, the edifice suffers from an apse of memory.

The young lad couldn't get married in his girlfriend's church because he belonged to a different abomination.

'At what age were you married?'
'At the parsonage.'

There is an admonitory notice outside one of London's churches which says: 'Are you going to sleep with the wise virgins, or wake with the foolish ones?'

And it's not only the Church of England that falls victim to the punster ...

The apprentice stonemason had just completed a monument to Baal. 'Now what shall I do?' he asked his boss. 'Don't worry, lad,' the boss assured him. 'The Devil makes work for idol hands.'

Would a dozen Jews together constitute a Jewry?

He could tell she was a Gentile soul from the goy expression on her face.

Philosophical puns range from those incorporating the names of prominent philosophers to those which are homespun pieces of philosophical advice. For example:

As René Descartes wrote, 'I fink, therefore I am.'

Kant was a German philosopher who devised the philosophy of Negativism. In fact, it was once said of him that 'If Immanuel Kant, then the Aga Kahn.'

Puns falling into the category of homespun advice include:

There are two kinds of people: married and cynical.

To be or not to be. What is the question?

Chalet or shanty? It's a decision he should dwell on.

The eternal triangle is usually right tangled.

Only organic gardeners till it like it really is.

The trouble with being inhibited is that you are so tied up in nots.

Counsel to old maids: better elate than never.

'It isn't often that I risk an argument with my wife, because when I do, words flail me!'

If there are plenty more pebbles on the beach, why haven't I had a shingle offer?

When the platform collapsed in the middle of his lecture, the professor picked himself up and sighed, 'Some dais are like that!'

A man wanted to buy his wife some of her favourite flowers, anemones. He called into the florist's, but found that all they had were a few stems of feathery ferns. Reluctantly, he bought these. He took them home and presented them, rather shamefacedly, to his wife. 'Never mind, darling,' she said. 'With fronds like these, who needs anemones!'

As the philosophical dentist said, 'The tooth will out!'

As the philosophical mother said to her young son at bath-time, when he got soap up his nose, 'Ah well, that's life, boy!'

A philosopher is like a looking-glass: he reflects.

From philosophy to politics. A few simple definitions of political terms:

Atrophy is a reward for long political service.

A bulldozer is a person who sleeps through party political broadcasts.

Excretory: a former Greek politician.

Liability is the measure of a politician.

Before most politicians get into office, someone has to vote for them.
If you don't know how to vote, just X someone.

The important thing is to vote, even if you don't know Y.

Before they are elected, politicians stand for office (in Great Britain) or they run for office (in the USA); and then, if elected, they sit in Parliament or Congress. And quite often, they go out on a limb to say some of the things they say, when they haven't really got a leg to stand on.

The queen dissolved Parliament, and then took the solute.

American politics ...
The visitor to an integrated American kindergarten was giving a speech to the class. 'Above all,' he concluded, 're-member that we are all Americans and because we are all Americans, we are all free!' A little black boy at the back of the class put up his hand. 'Excuse me, sir,' he lisped politely. 'I am not free.' 'Oh?' asked the visitor, taken aback. 'And why not?' 'Please, sir, I'm four.'

After the Watergate affair, many American politicians found themselves living by the law of the bungle.

To prove that punsters have no bias, for or against America, when they invent puns on American subjects, here are some counterbalancing Russian ones:
Communism is the opiate of the asses.

Lenin's tomb is a Communist plot.

If and when Russia again becomes a monarchy, the leader will probably be a Commie czar.

Communism can be measured by its nyet effect.

The existence of superpowers in the nuclear age gives rise to thoughts such as these:
One of the advantages of nuclear warfare is that all men are cremated equal.

Nuclear warfare is better than the old, fuzzy kind.

Some while ago, the following report was spotted in the press:
The Manx Government plans to relax regulations on boarding-houses to make more beds available for tourist sin late August and September.

A random few just to complete this section:
As the judge was in chambers,
He was inconvenienced by my request
And I have to see him
At his convenience.
It's such a potty system.

Cavalry motto: the best manoeuvre is horse manoeuvre.

When all the troops were mustard, the enemy turned yellow.

The Persian fleet at Salamis got so jittery waiting for the expected Athenian attack that they passed the word around:
Beware of skiffs bearing Greeks!

A warning-sign seen outside an apartheid-conscious South African sports arena said: The Wrestlers are Native Tonight.

3

AROUND THE WORLD IN EIGHTY WAYS

Let's start in England, and then go on to the rest of the United Kingdom, and then tackle some European puns. The rest of the world will come after that.

Did you know that there is a mysterious circle of stones at Stonehenge – but no one knows who Druid?

Kew is what tourists do to gain admission to a national botanical garden in London.

Said the Leaning Tower of Pisa to Big Ben, 'If you've got the time, I've got the inclination!'

A sign carried by an Arsenal supporter at the 1979 FA Cup final said: Show Us Your Cheek, Arsenal!

Is 'The Londonderry Air' a vulgar song about Londoners feeling a little behind?

To be accepted at Oxford, you must be both a gentleman and a sculler.

England not only has a blood bank, it also has a Liverpool.

The car-dealer goes to Bangor every day to buy old cars, and then Wrexham.

Would an early morning stroll along the sea-front make you Brighton cheery?

You can always tell if a lass is from Scotland by the way she rolls her Rs.

When fighting flares up in Belfast, the malicious called out.

You would think that their constant conflicts would someday lead the Irish to see the Eire of their ways.

And now we're in Europe, so:
Watch where European!

Commemorative tablets and statues have left many a European town epoch-marked.

First stop, France:
The murderer lured the girl to the top of the Eiffel Tower and then threw her in the river. As a result, she went insane.

For the tourist, Paris offers many attractive views. That's why the most famous tower there is called an Eiffel.

If English printers sing in quires,
Do French ones sing in reams?

When some Spaniards tried to flee to France over a single open bridge, they found that they had put all their Basques in one exit.

That last one is a reminder that Ex-Beatle John Lennon once wrote a book called *A Spaniard in the Works*.

Venice is an Italian interrogative, as in 'Venice the next gondola, please?'

Sign seen on a fast-food stall at the foot of the Leaning Tower of Pisa: Get a piece o' Pisa pizza here!

An Alpine hydroelectric scheme presumably produces off-peak electricity.

Warsaw the bombing of Poland.

Two hitch-hikers started off from London, heading for Turkey. One night, they stopped off in Bulgaria's capital city. Remarked one hitch-hiker to his pal, 'Sofia, so good!'

Typical British remarks made about the climate in the Greek isles are: Cor! Phew!

The Greeks may have invented the deep frieze, but they didn't think the idea worth Parthenon.

America:
'They grow so much wheat in Iowa that the farmers there are called cornographers.' 'That's amazing! Whatever will they think of next?'

The man from Miami – if you think his jacket is florid, you should see his wife's. It's even Florida!

You can always tell a baby from Alabama because it has a southern drool.

Hollywood's not-so-eternal triangles usually end up as wreck tangles.

There is a dress shop in Beverly Hills, California, called My Flair Lady. And there's a barber's shop in Chicago, Illinois, called US Hair Force.

A girl in New York was telling her girlfriend to beware of boys from the Windy City. The advice she gave: 'The boys from Chicago'll annoy.'

There's an old tramp who stands on Fifth Avenue in New York, and who makes a pretty penny being a habitué. He stands by a set of scales on the pavement, chanting to the passers-by, 'Habitué 165, habitué 184, habitué 126 . . .'

A man recently arrived in New York from Rome. He was in a large department store and found it necessary to approach the gentleman at the store's information desk. 'You tella me, please, where issa da rest room?' The man at the information desk pointed to the left and answered politely, 'Escalator, sir.' 'Escalator!' echoed the indignant Italian. 'Hell, mister, I gotta go now!'

A lady tourist at an Indian reservation noticed a swarm of children playing outside one tepee. 'How many children do you have?' she asked the father of the brood. 'Twenty-one,' he replied proudly. 'My, my!' reacted the lady tourist. 'Don't you have endless squabbles and fights and arguments?' 'Not at all,' grunted the Indian. 'We're just one big Hopi family!'

Did you know that the first inhabitants of North America were Orientals who came across from Asia once they got their bearing straight?

A gnome is a resident of one of Alaska's main towns.

After a major earthquake in northern California, a group of concerned local citizens set up the San Andreas Fund, which only goes to prove that some Americans can be generous to a fault.

Canada:
An old prospector was stranded in the Rockies and was desperately in need of water. He stumbled on a dry stream bed,

and then another, and yet another. He said bitterly, 'This is what I call going from one ex-stream to another!'

A man in Canada was charged with pulling a woman along the street by her hair. The magistrate asked the policeman, 'Was she drugged?' 'Yes, sir,' answered the policeman. 'Two whole blocks!'

Meanwhile, back in Central and South America:
What's the question his friends ask after a teenage boy's blind date? 'Jamaica?'

A group of Cuban delegates going to a convention were expelled on arriving at Santiago. It was reported that they got a Chile reception.

In his 1930 film *Animal Crackers*, Groucho Marx said:
'You go Uruguay, and I'll go mine!'

The peasant worker went to see his doctor, and told him that his right hand was Paraguay-ized and so he would need a few days off work. Replied the doctor, 'I Bolivia, but your boss won't!'

The rest of the world . . .
'How are you enjoying your visit to Africa?'
'Well, safari, so good!'

At Christmas time in Africa, Santa Claus arrives accompanied by jungle belles.

In the Middle East there's trouble brewin' – Things are going from Iraq to ruin.

Why will no men starve in the deserts of Arabia?
Because of the sand which is there!

How did you catch that Persian plane?
Iran!

The Tower of Babel was a din of iniquity.

A Turkish clerk, feeling the effects of too much drink, moaned to his lunchtime companion, 'We can't go back to the office now in this condition. Who'll tell the Bosphorus?'

'We've reached the end of the canal,' the voyager Said.

Did you know that a Siamese twin
Is someone with a strong family Thai?

Or that a Chinese voyeur is called a Peking Tom?

Or that Calcutta is an Indian butcher?

Or that Baghdad is an ageing bride's father?

Question: What is a crick?
Answer: The noise made by a Japanese camera.

Perhaps it was just the vodka Russian to my head that confused me!

Let's Finnish all these place-name puns with this specimen:
Waitress: 'Hawaii, mister, you must be Hungary.'
Customer: 'Yes, Siam. And I can't Rumania long, either. Venice lunch going to be ready?'
Waitress: 'I'll Russia table. What are you Ghana Havre? Do you want Aix?'
Customer: 'You want Tibet? I prefer Turkey. Would Jamaica cook step on the Gaza bit, please?'
Waitress: 'Odessa laugh! Alaska, but you'll hear her Wales!'

Customer: 'I'm not Balkan. Just put a Cuba sugar in my Java.'

Waitress: 'Don't be Sicily. Sweden it yourself. I'm only here to Serbia.'

Customer: 'Denmark my Czech, and call the Bosphorus. Egypt me. There's an Eire. I hope he'll Kenya. I don't Bolivia know who I am.'

Waitress: 'Canada noise! I don't Caribbean. You sure Ararat!'

Customer: 'Samoa your wisecracks? What's got India? Do you think this arguing Alps business? Why be so Chile? Be Nice!'

Waitress: 'Don't Kiev me that Boulogne! Pay your Czech and don't Kuwait. Abyssinia!'

Customer: 'I shan't be back, and I'll tell all my France not to come here!'

Gosh! How they Babylon!

Other geographical features . . .

No two pictures of forests are the same, although there may be similarity in the coppice.

When the visitor to the village was finally persuaded to visit the brook, he was somewhat dismayed to see it all emanating from a metal pipe. He protested that it was nothing more than a sewer. 'But,' his host relied, 'you can't tell a brook by its cover!'

The girl threatened to throw herself off a 700-foot cliff, but it turned out to be a big bluff.

On your first trip to the beach, you may find you'll get more sun than you basked for.

When rain falls, it gets up again in dew time.

A newspaper reported happily that a yachtsman feared lost in a violent Pacific storm had been found safe and cheerful. Said the paper, 'He had been shipwrecked on the shores of an uninhibited island.'

Is a tour de force a spell overseas with the Army?

A popular theory concerning the earth's creation: it was hot 'ere.

4

OHM'S PUN PHILOSOPHY

There are puns on the names of chemical elements and compounds; there are puns on different branches of science; there are puns on the names of scientists; and there are puns on the names of scientific instruments and devices.

A compound is a comical combination of two or more elements.

In French, the chemical term for water is H_2 eau.

The Archbishop of York once said, 'My ignorance of science is such that if anyone mentioned copper nitrate, I should think he was talking about policemen's overtime!'

Question: Where does mercury come from?
Answer: H.G. Wells.

The chemist was asked by his company to work on a new range of acetates, but he refused, knowing full well that he who acetates is lost.

Scientific measures department . . .
When you want your team to make a power play, you should erg them on!

Kilobars are what they put up at the windows of the prison cells where they keep murderers.

What did the physicist say when told he was going to be introduced to Farrah Fawcett-Majors?
I'm just dyne to metre.

The physicist had a recurrent pain in his back, and so went to see his doctor. The doctor asked his patient the frequency with which the pain came and went. But the physicist just replied, 'It hertz.'

As the electrician said, round about noon, 'I'm just going ohm for me lunch!'

As the electrician said in the middle of a wiring job, 'I'll just pop out to my van for some more wire. I won't be a mho.'

And some more electrical ones . . .
Did you hear about the political-minded ion who, hearing there was going to be an electron, went to the poles and volted?

Anode is a shocking piece of poetry created by a positive Pole.

Don't put too many adaptors into one socket; they confuse!

'At last I've got my radio working well,' said the radio ham ex-statically.

Hydroelectric plants in high mountains produce off-peak electricity. With the present energy crisis, every little bit Alps!

The prisoner is currently in a cell in a state of shock. He's waiting faraday for the circuit judge because he's charged with battery on the Tube. Although he conducts himself well and offers no resistance, he refuses all food and asks, 'Wire my insulate? I want to go ohm. Watt have I done? It wasn't my volt!'

Perhaps he was a terminal case!

Nuclear physics, rockets and robots are all punworthy subjects . . .

A nuclear physicist went away on a vacation. In his absence, he hung a sign on his Laboratory door. It said simply: Gone Fission.

Question: Do you know what would happen if you swallowed uranium?
Answer: You'd get a-tomic ache!

As the Martian explained on landing: 'We're here by accident. We didn't planet this way.'

Is a solitary sunspot a solar performance?

If God was playing poker, would he make a cosmic rays?

Man is gradually overcoming the problem of gravity, which is encouraging in view of the gravity of his problem.

Other sciences . . .
Forestry is fast becoming a poplar science.

A biologist boasted of changing the behaviour pattern of rats. In fact, he claimed to be pulling habits out of rats.

The United States National Bureau of Standards reports that there are ten million different colours. Hue can take your choice.

During the Depression in the USA, a scientist found a job skinning eels in a Government laboratory. He was contributing to the Nude Eel!

Why did the germ cross the microscope?
To get to the other slide.

Rocks that have been around for a long time are often taken for granite.

We live on a triangular estate. I think we've got the right angle, but you should see some of the squares on the other two sides.

And if you want some puns on scientific equipment:
Is a tired physicist a lazer?

As the poet-physicist scrawled on a wall:
Metre Rules, OK?

The radio ham was building his own radio telescope. Unfortunately, he needed many hundreds of one particular component. So he rushed down to his local radio components shop. The ham asked the proprietor for the components, and was dismayed to see that only a dozen were put on the counter. 'I want more than that,' cried the ham. 'But there antenna more left,' retorted the proprietor.

Advice given to the celibate youth who was ogling a particularly attractive girl: resistor!

There was a meteorologist who went mad and said forest

fires affect the Earth's weather. He proposed that all forests should be set on fire as this would permanently improve the climate. But his colleagues knew that weather satellite or not, the climate wouldn't change.

Did you hear about the computer entrepreneur who tried to make a fortune out of silicon chips? Apparently he went bust! It's not surprising in these inflated times!

And finally in this chapter:
Much science fiction offers us a horrorscope for the future.

5

TRANSPORTS OF DELIGHT

Big cars, small cars, fast cars, slow cars, expensive cars, and cheap cars, all designed to send us into transports of delight.

I'd like to buy a new car, but don't have the motorvation.

In fact, these days they don't make cars like they auto.

Of course, if you are thinking of buying a car, you might try a Ford or saloon.

Don't get Cortina trap and buy the most expensive model without an engineer's test, though Datsun other expensive item Honda bill if he fixes his Fiat a high level; cheaper to buy a boat and Citröen it if there Renault engines in it. Maybe you'll just have to Opel lower-priced model will come out.

If you want to buy a Swedish car, you ought to get a Fjord.

Though you might not believe it, most car manufacturers are more advanced than Ford. After all, it wasn't too long ago that Ford added a Ghia to its cars.

At Ford Motor Company's testing grounds, all prototype motor cars are identified by letters. Last year, models A through to R were failures, but you should have seen the escargot!

Next year, Ford will be making the model T. In fact, it's so new, it's still something of a Novel T.

If these puns start to read like an advertisement for Ford, let's move on to some other makes:

It takes a lot of bread to own a Rolls.

He used to have a Singer Chamois. It was a deer little car; he had it from gnu.

Did you hear about the car that Renault de petrol?

As the American motor manufacturer said, 'You have to be smart if you want to make a fast Buick.'

'I used to have a Pathfinder.' 'Oh, Riley!'

I've often wondered how it feels to take a girl home and then kiss her goodnight standing on her Porsche!

German cars have excellent roadholding ability. You should see them on the Benz!

I always thought that the Wolseley was a cardinal car.

If you want a fancy vehicle, though, you mustn't expect it to be Jeep!

Question: Which car will give the best mileage?
Answer: Your gas is as good as mine!

Drive on . . .

If you just want something to drive around the farm, this carrot to do it!

They've designed a new vehicle intended only for coping with traffic during the rush hour. It's called a stationary wagon.

No expert on motorway speeds,
Sober or with cider.
In the graveyard now his headstone reads,
'He crossed the Great Divider.'

'You're a good driver,' she said automatically. 'I only made a ewe turn,' he replied somewhat sheepishly.

One of the trusties at a prison farm in the southern USA roused the warden from his bed, shouting, 'There's a convict outside attaching an aeroplane propeller to your old jalopy! I think he's preparing to fly the coupé!'

Back-seat driving is a form of duel control.

Parking a yellowish-brown car in the desert is fine, as long as when you come back, you can find the khaki.

Some drivers are very ill-tempered and inclined to be pugnacious. They just can't wait to reach a duel carriageway!

You may find that teaching your wife to drive will drive you round the bend.

Cars don't just take you from A to B. Sometimes they just stay at C...
Is a drive-in movie autoerotic?

One night, a car pulled up beside a van parked on a lonely road. The kindly car driver called out, 'Out of petrol?' 'Nope!' 'Tyre down?' 'Nope! Didn't have to!'

A sign seen in a car scrapyard in London simply said: 'Rust in Peace.'

Having relations in a car can be an uncomfortable experience, especially if you're both on the back seat.

Is an autobiography a history of motor cars?

Is autoeroticism the love of motor cars?

Tyre-repair charges vary enormously. It would be much better if all garages had a flat rate.

Head lice are what you find on the front of a car. In the dark, they help you find your way from hair to there.

A rectangle is the result of a head-on collision.

Modern roads have evolved into the arrival of the fittest.

Spaghetti Junction is a kind of crossroad puzzle.

Down to the sea:
A famous Egyptian boat-builder became known as the fez that launched a thousand ships.

Even before oars were invented, Spaniards were able to go for thousands of miles on a galleon.

The boy stood on the burning deck
Whence all but he had fled.
It was a hull of a spot to be in.

The president of a large bank fell off a seagoing yacht. While his friends frantically looked for a lifejacket, a sailor shouted, 'Hey, can you float alone?' 'Of course I can,' gasped the floundering banker, 'but this is a hell of a time to talk business!'

Ordered to help row the lifeboat, the first-class passenger sniffed, 'Do I have a choice?' 'Certainly, sir,' replied a sailor. 'Either oar.'

Flights of fancy:
Is a palindrome a friend waiting for you at the airport?

The control tower at a large airport radioed to a pilot that he had a hole in the bottom of his fuel tank, and that he was to fly upside down to prevent it from spilling. 'Hurry up!' the message warned. 'Loop before you leak!'

If British Rail introduce more no-smoking compartments, will it reduce the incidence of Pullmanry complaints?

The British Rail service to Bury is presumably Inter City.

Is a blunderbuss a vehicle used for random travel?

As the old proverb says: A bird in the hand is worth two in the bus.

A tantrum is a two-seated bicycle.

Back in the horse-and-cart days, the country really had a stable economy.

The pretty young thing had a boyfriend who was a taxi-driver. He was tall, tanned and good-looking. But the thing that she admired most about him was his hansom carriage.

Travelling by flying carpet is a rugged experience.

Refuel here . . .

'Shall I check under the bonnet?' asked the attendant politely. 'No thanks,' replied the car owner. 'Oil be all right!'

In these days of increasing oil shortages, many home-owners are reverting to using coal, recognizing that there's no fuel like an old fuel.

'We've struck oil!' gushed the petroleum engineer.

If the Arabs are getting fatter, why is their gasoline?

Rear end . . .

Sign seen on a tyre shop: We Skid You Not.

Sign seen outside a garage specializing in accident repairs: May We Have the Next Dents, Please?

Question: How far can a spook travel?
Answer: From ghost to ghost!

Traffic slogan: Children should be seen and not hurt!

6

ANIMAL MAGIC

Two general observations before we deal with specific animals:
Even the most primitive of animals has an elementary canal.

A caucus is a dead animal.

Let's look at the animals in alphabetical order.
Aardvark is just heavy labour. 'It's aardvark, but it pays pretty well!'

A shampoo is an impostor bear.

'Do you hunt bear?'
'Not in cold weather!'

'Has he ever tried to tell you about his forebears?'
'Gracious, no! Don't tell me he's an animal trainer.'

A brontosaurus is an anthology of works by nineteenth-century sister authors called Charlotte, Emily and Anne.

Buffalo is a greeting used between two nudists.

To get ahead in the early days of America's pioneer west, many a man had to beg, burro and steal.

This time, our cat has really gone too fur, and has got pregnant. As purr usual.

There was this cat that was a rather pathetic sight, and it was several degrees below purr. It was always getting in people's way. When people stepped on it, its felines were hurt.

Our dog got fleas, but our catgut kittens.

A cheetah is a kind of Indian leopard trained to hunt deer. Unfortunately, you just can't trust it.

Not all cows are contented creatures. The other day, one muttered to her farmer, 'Go ahead and milk me! See if I give a dram!'

Farmer Giles once had a psychotic cow. Everything that he told her went in one ear and out the udder. Apparently she had a fodder complex.

He was like a bull in a china shop until she cowed him.

An elderly couple possessed a few farmyard animals and a single, very lean cow. Even though the cow never gave milk, the old couple loved her. After a long illness, the cow eventually died. Mourned the sad couple, 'Thin cow, we loved her.'

When you're selling cows, it's often a byre's market.

When both cow-milkers claimed to have won hands down, the cow-milking contest ended in udder chaos.

Did you hear about the cowboy who had 300 cows? He thought he only had 297 until he rounded them up.

A dog always finds forfeit better than two.

'Stop hounding me,' he barked.

He went to the costume party as a dog, and found himself curtailed.

Rough: this was what the dog said when it sat on the sandpaper.

'Where have you been?' she asked.
'Out walking the dog,' he replied. 'Looking for the old familiar faeces.'

The Black Knight had lost his horse. (Some say it caught a colt!) He called in at the local stable to pick up a new horse, but found that all the horses had gone. The stable-keeper told him that the only animal left was a mangy old dog, and that the knight could have that if he wished. The Black Knight was most offended at the suggestion. 'You shouldn't send a knight out on a dog like this,' he chided.

Aspersion: a donkey from Iran.

A famous elephant was the unquestioned leader of the forest. Being a benign dictator, he decided that one day he would teach his subjects about agriculture. He imported machinery, including a forklift that also doubled as a mechanical plough. The animals were hard to train, though. One leopard, rather long in the tooth, insisted on using an old hoe to work the potatoes and air them. 'Why are you continuing to do it the old way? enquired the elephant. The leopard answered, 'It's the only way I know to aerate the soil round the spuds.' 'Hell, that's old-fashioned,' chastened the elephant. 'Now watch me carefully,' he continued. Whereupon the elephant clambered up on the mechanical plough and, going down the rows, showed how easy and heavenly it could be with a machine doing the work. 'Do you get the idea?' enquired the elephant of the old leopard. 'To air is human, but to forklift, divine!'

Groan,groan!

Siamese twins occur most often among humans; for example, you very rarely see a double ewe.

As one ram said to the other, 'After ewe.'

Or as the girl goat said to the boy goat, 'I don't mind going out with you, but please don't kid me.'

Mountain goats is a sexual perversion. They're so horny anyway.

Bambi could never have been a mother
If her hart hadn't been in the right place.

Question: What weighs 1,500 kilos and wears flowers in its hair?
Answer: A hippiepotamus

Three Indian squaws were admitted to the reservation's maternity ward at the same time. The obstetrician asked one of the squaws to lie on a buffalo hide, the second to lie on an elk hide, and the third to lie on a hippopotamus hide. The squaws on the elk and buffalo hides each produced a seven-pound son. But the squaw on the hippopotamus hide mothered healthy seven-pound twins. All of which proves, of course, that the sons of the squaw on the hippopotamus equal the sons of the squaws on the other two hides.

How can it be proved that a horse has six legs? Just count them: he has forelegs in front and two behind!

'The stallion has gone wild,' he said hoarsely.

Many horses feel a bit down in the mouth.

A horse farm made it a habit to bottle-feed its colts when they were only a few days old.

Hence: a foal and his mummy are soon parted.

The zoo's kangaroo lacks energy. He is frequently discovered out of bounds.

The zoo's baby kangaroo was asked why it wouldn't jump into the adult kangaroo's pouch. 'I can't,' the baby explained. 'It's not my bag!'

The animal trainer sighed. 'That leopard is too quarrelsome. There's no hope of that catamountain to anything!'

Is a chimpanzee a gay monkey?

Do unto otters as you would have them do unto you.

When colonies of pigs attack each other, is it just a replay of the Boar War?

The Russian's wife told him that it was snowing outside, but he disagreed. He thought that it was rain rather than snow. As he observed to his wife, 'Rudolph the Red knows rain, dear!'

A New York investor saw an advertisement offering a stock market newsletter from Australia. Willing to try anything to change his luck, he subscribed. When the first issue arrived, it contained just four words: Buy sheep, sell deer.

There is a whale who has retired from work at Marineland, Florida. But he still hangs around, cadging food from tourists. In fact, he's becoming a real ne'er-do-whale.

In Tibet, a yak accidentally wandered into a deep pit where rubble was being burned. Of course, the yak started to sizzle. It was some while before a native, the yak's owner, discovered the tragedy. Gazing on the scene, he cried to himself, 'Oh, my baking yak!'

Question: What's black and white and red all over?
Answer number 1: A newspaper.
Answer number 2: An embarrassed zebra.

But then a zebra is a horse of a different choler.

No sweeter girl ewe ever gnu
Than Betty Marten's daughter Sue.
With sable hair, small tapir waist,
And lips you'd gopher miles to taste;
Bright, lambent eyes, like the gazelle,
Sheep pertly brought to bear as well;
Ape pretty lass, it was avowed,
Of whom her marmot to be proud.
Deer girl! I loved her as my life,
And vowed to heifer for my wife.

'I'm not particularly fond of snakes,' he rattled.

Shortly after the pregnant snake swallowed the rubber ball, she gave birth to a bouncing baby boa.

When the zookeeper discovered that his boa constrictor had escaped, he hung a sign on the cage, which said: Gone to Crunch.

When the Great Flood had abated Noah sent the animals off the Ark, enjoining each couple to 'go forth and multiply'. As he was clearing up afterwards, he came upon two snakes. 'I thought I told you to go forth and multiply,' he exclaimed.

'We're sorry, sir, but we can't,' one of them replied. 'You see, sir, we're adders!'

'I hate birds' he groused.

Birds make such tweet music!

Question: Why did the chicken cross the road?
Answer: For fowl reasons.

Is a smart duck a wise quacker?

The baby owl was just learning to talk. It kept saying 'What? What?' until its wise old father explained, 'Son, it's not "what" you know, it's "who" you know!'

Aviaries are such cheep places.

If a swan sings its swan song, does a young swan sing its cygneture tune?

While most of the flock settled on trees or power lines, one crow always headed for telephone wires. Once there, he seemed to spend all his time talking to himself. Another crow finally asked him why he did this. 'Oh,' said the gabby one, 'I just like to make long-distance caws.'

Is a chandelier a French rooster?

'What happens when geese fly upside down?'
'They quack up!'

Old vaudeville repartee: 'You wanna viaduct?'
'Viaduct?' 'It's cheaper than a goose!'

Weather vane or not, he's certainly cocky!

The trustees of the Madrid Zoo read that there were only thirty whooping cranes left in the USA, and they decided that they must have one before the birds became extinct. A bird was soon dispatched by air freight. Alas, when the silly bird arrived, it flatly refused to be unloaded. The moral of this story is that cranes in Spain stick mainly to the plane!

To keep in trim, some birds have taken to dancing. You can quite often see a couple of flamingo dancers in our local park.

'If eider choice, eider taken up ornithology,' he crowed.

Some birds can be very ungainly. In fact, some are auk-ward, and others can be even more hawk-ward.

The Christmas dinner was very well cooked; it was done to a tern.

Being afraid of felines, the Australian bird cassowary eye when he hears emu.

Some puns are fishier than others . . .
'But I don't like fish,' he said in a bass voice.

Why can you never expect a fisherman to be generous?
Because his business makes him sell fish.

When a man in Japan has to choose between fishing and farming, he usually puts the carp before the horse.

Young fish like to play carps and robbers.

'Do you have much in your creel?' the returning fisherman was asked, 'Oh, yes, a good eel!'

There was once a fisherman in the Gulf of Mexico who

caught an eel in which he found a very large diamond ring. He sold the ring and then retired on his eel-gotten gains.

If someone tends to carp, don't let him chub you around.

It strikes me that anyone who is a dab hand at a thing has something fishy about him.

Now that Britain's rivers are getting cleaner, happy dace are here again.

The independent fish proclaimed, 'I am not my brother's kipper!'

There is a fishing boat down in Cornwall which has bumpers fore and aft. To the enquiring tourist, the captain explains that they are shark absorbers.

The fisherman's song: 'To Dream the impossible Bream.'

First dolphin: 'What did you say when you bumped into that bully dolphin?'
Second dolphin: 'I just told him that I didn't do it on porpoise.'

In a fishmonger's shop, the fish are usually displayed in roes.

One worm to another, on meeting in a Dover sole, 'What's a nice girl like you doing in a plaice like this?'

The fisherman didn't enjoy his breakfast. He was hard of herring.

When salmon swim upstream, they have to salmon up a lot of effort.

He was a piano tuna, even though he couldn't play a newt!

When the fisherman died, they thought he might have been poisoned, but it turned out to be an act of cod!

Two Englishmen, alone in London for an evening, were discussing what to do. 'Shall we go to the flicks?' one suggested. 'They're showing Moby Dick.' 'No, thanks,' exclaimed the other. 'I detest sex films.' 'Oh, but this is about whales!' 'Even worse,' his friend said with a shudder. 'I can't stand Welshmen!'

What did the protoplasm say to the amoeba?
Don't bacilli!

What do bees do with their honey? They cell it.

Two boll weevils decided to give up farming and try their luck in the big city. One of them married the daughter of a rich termite and had a boll. The other failed at everything he tried, and became known as the lesser of two weevils.

Termites are boring; they work with all termite.

'You're always telling lice ant you mite be found out,' he ticked her off.

Pondered the introverted worm to itself, 'What's life all about? What'll become of me? Worm I going?'

7

TINKER, TAILOR, SOLDIER, SAILOR

Tinker, tailor, soldier, sailor, rich man, poor man, beggarman, thief. Even if they're not all in here, lots of their fellow workers are ...

As the actor in the travelling roadshow admitted, 'I am what I ham!'

Is it necessary to have a small actor to play Hamlet?

A true ad-man
Writes the prose
And cons.

The convicted architect soon discovered that the prison walls were not built to scale.

The figures that the artist painted were distorted pastel recognition.

The artist's pictures are atmospheric.
He paints by nimbus.

The soldier's wartime dream: being with a squad of eighty yes-girls!

Pleasant-faced people are generally the most welcome, but the auctioneer is always pleased to see a man whose appearance is for bidding.

A bachelor is an unaltared male.

Many a bachelor feels the need to insert his masculinity.

An eccentric bachelor passed away and left a nephew nothing but 5,000 clocks. The nephew now works full-time winding up the estate.

As a bank manager, my only interest is to get you a loan and make advances.

German barbers like to be dressed formally. Accordingly, they should always be greeted as 'Herr Dresser'.

The sunburn season is ushered in by the peeling of the belles.

'Mah deah,' drawled the southern belle to her overweight friend, 'you-all look simply divan.'

He's a fair boxer. His swing can make a round a bout.

I'm learning to steal. A cat burglar is teaching mioaw.

The candlemakers are pressuring their employers for longer wick ends.

Did you hear about the cellist who lost her job through making her scherzo short?

Said a provincial newspaper in reporting a story about a local pensioner: 'They thought she was ninety-nine, but are now convinced that she is a centurion.'

He advertised for a limousine but had nothing to chauffeur it.

A receptionist at the Miami Hilton called the hotel detective. 'There's something odd going on with the man in room 509. Would you check?' When the detective returned to the lobby, the clerk asked, 'Well, did you find any of the hotel's towels in his suitcase?' 'No,' said the detective, 'but I found a chambermaid in his grip.'

As the clown said when a nun watching the circus parade from her balcony fell on him, 'This is virgin on the ridiculous!'

I never had much respect for the army. I always thought that colonels were nuts.

Did you hear about the two coin collectors who got together just for old dimes' sake?

A witty American columnist once described an unhappy millionairess as 'that poor little wretch girl'.

I've heard that to become a coroner you have to take a stiff examination.

Going to the dentist can be a drilling experience.

It's very easy for a dermatologist to build up his practice. He just starts from scratch.

A film director wanted to do a picture about eunuchs, but he couldn't get his budget approved because of the cast ration.

Is a divorcee a woman who gets richer by decrees?

When his lordship's crew mutinied during a storm, the first thing they did was to pour the earl on troubled waters.

The chief of the cannibals asked his captive what his occupation was. 'I am an editor.' 'Congratulations!' exclaimed the head cannibal. 'Tomorrow you will be editor in chief!'

'We have no room for such a lengthy obituary,' moaned the city editor. 'It must be cut down to proper die-mention.'

Royalty can be pretty empressive.

Did you know that the entrepreneur is a vying breed?

'This will be over in necks to no time,' said the executioner.

If you want to get ahead as an executioner, just axe for some information.

Last week, a fire-eater made the front pages of the national newpapers. His flame was spreading.

You may have heard that the fish-processing factory had a vacancy, but I couldn't fillet.

Quote from an arrested forger: 'I wasn't much of a salesman, but I mint well.'

A fortune-teller gazed into his crystal ball and burst into laughter. His young lady client rose and smacked his face. 'Why did you do that?' asked the amazed clairvoyant. Said the girl firmly, 'My mother always told me to strike a happy medium.'

Is a livelihood an active gangster?

Is it true that only organic gardeners till it like it is?

You mustn't get too involved with gardening. Emotional gardeners are often overcome with bouts of wisteria.

A gentleman is someone who always offers a lady deceit.

When she was small
No one would fall,
But with her teens
Stretching her jeans,
The boys avow
That she's a beguile now.

Why do gypsies never become insane?
Because they lead nomad lives.

The reason that it's so hard to understand hippies is that you can't always hear a man who is talking below a whisker.

When he applied for the job of human cannonball, they took him like a shot.

The indiarubber man had a pretty poor social life. Every time he went to a party, he made an S of himself.

The king's jester punned incessantly, until the king, in desperation, condemned the jester to be hanged. However, when the executioners had taken the jester to the gallows, the king relented, thinking that after all a good jester was not easy to find. He sent a messenger post-haste with a royal pardon. Arriving at the gallows as the jester stood with the rope about his neck, the messenger read the king's decree: the jester would be pardoned if he would promise never to make another pun. The jester could not resist the temptation, however. He cackled out, 'No noose is good news.' And with that, he was hanged.

Judge: 'I'll fine you just ten dollars this time. But if it happens again tomorrow, I'll throw you into jail.'
Offender: 'I get it, Your Honour. Fine, today; cooler, tomorrow.'

A line from 'The Ballad of the Fallen Knight': 'It was joust one of those things.'

I fancied myself as a knight errant, but some other man had his armour round her.

As the divorce lawyer said when he met his newest and prettiest client at a party, 'May I evidence with you?'

Is a vandyke a truck-driving lesbian?

The chief librarian explained that the reason her library is not adding any more fairy tales to its collection is that it has run out of elf space.

As they went up to the twenty-second floor, he smiled his sexiest smile at the pretty lift operator and murmured, 'I'll bet all these stops and starts make you pretty worn out.' 'It's not the stops and starts that get me down,' she said. 'It's the jerks!'

Do lighthousekeepers have big families?
Yes, because they are always lots of gulls and buoys around.

'So you're a locksmith,' rumbled the judge. 'What has that to do with being in that gambling house when it was raided?' 'Well, you see, Your Honour, I was just making a bolt for the door.'

Is the theme song of the love-smitten manicurist 'Thanks for the Emery'?

The retired boxer refused a job at a massage parlour, because he didn't like to pull paunches.

The meteorologist admitted, 'We don't really know weather it will rain or shine.'

Coal miners are vein men.

The miner didn't know whether he had struck iron ore what.

After years of moving from one big mining job to another, the disgusted mining engineer finally exclaimed, 'Great mines stink alike!'

Show me an unemployed movie star and I'll show you a movie idle.

There was a British film called *Asylum* made in 1972. In one of the scenes, a murderer, after dismembering his wife, says to the remains, 'Rest in pieces.'

'Hey,' said one musician to another, 'who was that piccolo I saw you out with last night?' 'That was no piccolo, that was my fife.'

Nightwatchmen don't look liberated, yet they've been burning their braziers for years.

An old maid is one who will only go so far and no fervour.

Is a pedagogue a person who gets excited over feet?

A pessimist is a person who looks at the world through morose-coloured glasses.

A sign seen in the window of a cobbler's shop next to a medical centre: Physician, heel thyself!

In the world of nursing, physiotherapists are often referred to as physio (the rapists)!

'Well,' said the grounded pilot bitterly, 'if the fog lifts, it certainly won't be mist.'

First pirate: 'Not bad for a buccaneer!'
Second pirate: 'Two dollars.'
First pirate: 'Not bad for a bucanneer!'

In mid-1979 a Sunday newspaper advertised a flat for sale with 'hot and cold running porters'.

The hotel porter refused to carry my baggage, so I punched him.
My case comes up next week.

'It says here that a man over the road throttled his mother-in-law yesterday,' said the lady. 'Hhhmmm,' mused her husband, 'sounds to me like he was a practical choker.'

Three English professors, returning to their university, encountered a group of young women who were on the game. Having managed to evade them gracefully, one professor, a Shakespearean scholar, chuckled, 'What might one call such a congregation? A flourish of strumpets?' The second professor, whose special area was Anthony Trollope, understandably preferred 'a chapter of trollops'. But the winner was the third and youngest professor's nomination: 'an anthology of pros'.

The members of the oldest profession are not really lost women, they are just mislaid.

The police inspector was shown two sets of fingerprints of a suspected bank robber. 'These can't belong to the same man,' he protested. 'They're whorls apart.'

The psychiatrist told the fellow who said his girlfriend treated him like every other pebble on the beach that he would have to be a little boulder.

The sailor, he rants like an old sea-dog, but his barque is worse than his bight.

A photograph salesman makes more money by enlarge.

When the poetic French perfume salesman fell in love with a chambermaid, he gave her an ode de toilette.

For years, the travelling salesman had lavished his attention on the buxom showgirls of Las Vegas. He finally tried dating one of the less buxom girls, but she wouldn't let him leave the gambling tables. Which proved that she was only a little better.

A prospective tenant was being shown round a property by an attractive woman from the estate agents. Enquired the man, 'Are you to be let with the flat?' Responded the lady, 'No, sir, I'm to be let alone!'

'There's one difficult thing about taking dictation with my boss,' sighed the secretary. 'You have to take an awful lot for grunted!'

Is a group of trainee secret service agents aspiring?

A shoplifter is a shopper with the gift of the grab.

After years of constant practice, the singer finally came to a choir a good voice.

I've heard that a skier often jumps to contusions.

And that a speaker who needs no introduction is beyond compère.

Most fans of pop music are star-craving mad.

As the stamp collector said, 'Philately will get you everywhere.'

At a US Air Force base in the southern USA, a newly assigned colonel walked into his office and asked the pretty young secretary, 'What is the normal complement of this office?' 'Why, colonel,' exclaimed the girl, 'I reckon the most normal is "Howdy, honeypot, you sure are lookin' luscious this mornin'."'

While out walking in Richmond Park, a young lady heard for the first time of her mother's intention to remarry. She was obliged to sit right down and cry. She couldn't go a step farther.

When the semi-literate streetwalker unwittingly approached a member of the vice squad, her proposition ended with a sentence.

As the critic wrote of the stripper, 'Some things are better left unshed.'

I heard that the striptease artist got arrested in the middle of her act: her buff was called.

Is a retired supermarket employee called an exchequer?

When the headmistress asked the new English teacher how long she planned to teach, the reply was, 'From here to maternity.'

'How would you classify a telephone operator? Is it a business or a profession?' 'Neither, really. It's more of a calling!'

The new ship's choir was doing well with its opening numbers until the tenors got lost on the high Cs.

Two thieves in Casablanca mugged the town's richest citizen. As they made off with their loot, one observed to the other, 'We must do this Moor often.'

As the philosophical tightrope walker asked himself. 'Wire we here?'

She told me that she was just a travelling companion, but I sensed arrival.

Twins usually get along well with each other because they start out as wombmates.

Before the war an umpire, hated by everyone and brutal enough to beat his wife, finally decided to reform. One day, he asked his little boy to sit on his lap. But the boy refused. Why? Because the son never sits on the brutish umpire.

The poet Thomas Hood complained that a keen undertaker wanted 'to urn a lively Hood'.

As the weatherman said, 'Disgusting is going to come to blows.'

A wife is sometimes described as her husband's bitter half.

When the witch said 'abradacabra', nothing happened. She's a hopeless speller.

To be a good writer of detective stories, you need to run a clue factory.

The yachtsman bought his girlfriend a small bikini and watched her beam with delight.

A yes-man is one who stoops to concur.

Is there anyone who hasn't managed to get into this list? If so, the next two items are a kind of round-up.

His paper business folded,
His brassière business went bust,
His direct mail concern was written off,
His submarine company went under,
And his poster company went to the wall.

I'll be with you
in half a tick, said the vivisectionist
in two sex, said the hermaphrodite
in two shakes, said the freemason
in a trice, said the Third Man
in a flash, said the magician
in an instant, said the marketing man
in a wile, said the craftsman
in a twinkling, said eye

If lawyers can be disbarred, and priests can be unfrocked, how might people in other walks of life be drummed out of their profession or calling? Electricians might be delighted, poultry farmers might be delayed, and musicians might possibly be denoted! If cowboys can be deranged, then models can be deposed, and judges can be distorted. A clairvoyant who loses his or her licence would be dispirited, an executioner would be decapitated, and a jeweller would be dilapidated. You will be able to dream up plenty of these for yourself, but first check to see that they aren't in the following list.

Bankers are disinterested.
Butchers are delivered.
Models are denuded.
Songwriters are decomposed.
Castles are demoted.
Surveyors are dislocated.
Accountants are disfigured.
Witch doctors are dispelled.
Train drivers are derailed.
Symphony conductors are disconcerted.
Siamese twins are departed.
Diplomats are disconsolate.
Cannibal victims are disheartened.
Ministers are demoralised.
Orchestra leaders are disbanded.
Winemakers are deported.
Mathematicians are discounted.
Advertisers are declassified.
Martians are unearthed.
Violinists are unstrung.
Admirals are abridged.
Tailors are unsuited.
Neurologists are unnerved.
Brides are dismissed.
Committee members are disappointed.
Electricians get discharged.
Authors are described.
Choristers are unsung.
Mathematicians are nonplussed
Politicians are devoted.
Calendar makers are disMayed.
Hairdressers are distressed.
Tree surgeons are uprooted.
Prisoners are excelled.
Bridge players are discarded.
Teachers are outclassed.

Meteorologists are disgusted.
Turkey stuffers are undressed.
Eulogists are distributed.
Puzzlers are dissolved.
Clubs are dismembered.
Private eyes are undetected.
Botanists are deflowered.
Tennis players are unloved and defaulted!
Arsonists are unmatched and fired!
Gunsmiths, they're just plain fired!

8

DRESSED TO KILL

Skirts, dresses, bikinis, trousers, shirts, shoes, and sew on . . .
Women who wear fishnet tights are usually happy to shoal
their legs.

Sign seen in a window featuring one manufacturer's range of
brassières:
'*This is the real Decoy.*'

Is a cobra a brassière for Siamese twins?

Is a brassière a bust stop?

Many a girl has discovered too late that a sailor can be a wolf
in ship's clothing!

'There's surely one advantage to short skirts.'
'Yes?'
'They make it so much easier for girls to get up stares.'

Women with bad legs should stick to long skirts because they
cover a multitude of shins.

'Your dress is a little tight,' he said fittingly.

'How can I possibly wear such tight dresses!' she burst out.

A home-made dress often tends to look sew-sew.

A businessman in Hong Kong had a wife who spent all her time worrying about clothes. One night he arrived home to find her in tears. In exasperation, he demanded, 'What sarong now?'

Is battledress a tog of war?

I don't know about that, but the toga was the sack of Rome.

For girls in the country, shorts are the best high stile fashion.

Other women say she dresses like a tart, but she suits the guise.

Modern fashions are often presented with tongue in chic.

I'm a bit chicken where birds are concerned, but I somehow need less pluck if she's well dressed.

Material witness: she is often canvassed, but never suede.

The pressures of being in the fashion business are enough to drive any dress designer right round the trend.

Embarrassed: Emily's condition after losing her trousers.

When the slipper salesman had spent his last and was on his uppers, he cried, 'Well, that's shoe business!'

Negligent: is this a male version of a negligee?

'Mum makes me wear pants with patches on deceit.'

Two male silkworms were trying to score with a female silkworm, but they ended up in a tie.

When the crafty old sea-dog's boat sank, the first thing he did was dash to a haberdashery to buy a new yachting cap. The hatter asked sympathetically, 'Capsize?' Answered the tar, 'Seven and three-eighths!'

Some fences deal in antiques and jewellery, others enclose.

If you're going to rob a bank, wear a stocking mask. Denier won't be recognized.

One of the Sunday newspapers ran a special section on furs some time ago. It was entitled: 'Clothes Encounters of the Furred Kind.'

Never accept a fur unless it's in mink condition.

When the robbers held up the furrier's shop, the leader ran off with the cash and left his accomplice to take the wrap.

The gangster gave his girlfriend a mink stole for Christmas. 'Is it really a mink stole?' she gasped. 'Well, honey, I can't guarantee that it's genuine mink, but it sure is stole!'

A gambler in a casino came home richer by £2000 one night. Climbing into bed, he slipped the money under his pillow and remarked to his wife, 'In the morning, I'm going to buy you a mink coat.' Unfortunately, being excited about his success, he couldn't sleep, so he got up a little later, returned to the casino, and lost all of the money he had won. In the morning, his wife woke him early and said, 'Let's go and get that mink coat.' Her husband slid his hand under the pillow and sighed. 'Go back to sleep,' he mumbled. 'I don't feel two grand.'

The G-string worn by strippers is said to have derived its name from the exclamations of the audience.

The attributes of bathing suits
For lasses of lithesome limb
Make me enquire if this attire
Is worn to slink or swim.

'I'll slip into my bikini,' she said briefly

I told her no sensible man
Would take her dancing
In her bikini
So she went with a little moron.

'I just don't want to discuss your clothes allowance,' he said, skirting round the subject.

She tried to sell me some underwear, but I knew she had a vested interest.

Are fashionable shops that sell shoes called bootiques?

Some people like to get married early in the morning; morning suits them.

'I hat going into milliners' shops,' she cried.

9

OAT CUISINE

What's cooking . . .
Some cooks add a dash
Of this and that to hash.
Others feel they're too far gone
Just making sure the soupçon.

Brouhaha is a French term meaning 'the joy of cooking'.

In these days of rising oil costs, even cooking oil can lead to expense that is gastronomical.

He was so sure of his facts that he said he would eat his hat. Alas, many a true word is spoken ingest.

It was his last meal, but you should have seen how the assassinate.

'Eat all you want, there's extradition the pantry!'

When it comes to eating, Frenchmen are the real messrs.

Oat cuisine is what Scotsmen call porridge.

Russia has supplied samovar recipes.

Dinner was announced, soviet.

Overeating will make you thick to your stomach.

Goblin your food
Is bad for your elf.

Trying to preserve his *savoir faire* in a new restaurant, the guest looked down at the eggs the waiter had spilled on his lap and said brightly, 'Well, I guess the yolk's on me!'

'Dinosaur' is a term used in restaurants when complaints are received about the food or service. A question often asked is 'What made that dinosaur?'

Seen on the menu in a restaurant that specializes in low-calorie foods: 'Our dishes will take your breadth away.'

Slimmers' motto: here today, gaunt tomorrow.

Those who work for peanuts
Are always shelling out
And it's those with cashew
Can salt some away.

When Eve offered Adam an apple,
It was only then that they realized
They had no cloves.

'This can't be beet,' said the farmer as he pulled up a carrot.

Lady: 'You were cheated when you bought this diamond ring.'
Gent: 'I don't think so. I know my onions.'
Lady: 'Onions, maybe. Carats, no!'

'My dustbin's full of toadstools.'
'How do you know that?'
'Because there's not mushroom inside!'

I may be a lover of tropical tubers, but I yam what I yam.

My girlfriend is such a swede thing, with her radish cheeks and carroty hair.

Sign seen outside a fish and chip shop: 'We Fry Harder.'

'Tough luck,' cracked the egg in the monastery, 'Out of the frying pan, into the friar!'

When hard times came upon the monastery, the abbot decided to set up a fish and chip shop at the entrance. Brother Jonathan was put in charge of frying the fish, and Brother Leonard was put in charge of the spuds. The local citizens soon learned to ask for one man or the other when they wanted just fish or just chips. One night, a newcomer to the area went in. He wanted just fish, and said to the man behind the counter, 'I say, are you the fish friar?' 'No,' said Brother Leonard, 'I'm the chip monk.'

Most fish and chip shops in this area open at 7 p.m., but there's one, quite well-known, that doesn't open until 10.30, when the pubs turn out. They have a sign up behind the counter. It says: 'Batter late than never.'

A Leicestershire farmer with poor relatives in East Germany sent them a food package. Unfortunately, it got lost somewhere *en route*. When the farmer heard this, he wanted to set their minds at ease, so he sent them a telegram, 'Cheer up! The wurst is yet to come!'

When fire broke out in the meat factory, you never sausage a mess!

'This sausage really has a lot of flavour,' he remarked sagely.

'Hot dog!' he exclaimed with relish.

'You bring the sausages, and I'll bring a Canada best sauerkraut.'

Sign seen outside the stadium where stock car racing takes place every Friday evening: 'Bangers and Smash.'

'I just love cheese,' he said Kraft-ily.

You should never St Ivel a cheesemaker's ambitions.

First cheese advertisement: 'English Cheddar. Gorge-ous.'
Second advertisement: 'New Cheeseland Zeal.'

'Kiss me,' she whispered passionately. 'But I'm hungry,' he replied. 'Quiche me first.'

Car bow hide rates . . .
    'I can't eat starchy food,' he said stiffly.

The art of growing wheat, maize and corn is called cornography. (You 'ear some awful corn these days!)

If you go into a bakery that has just had an explosion, you are likely to find that the cause is a Napoleon blown apart.

A grain of wheat fell asleep in a field. When it woke up, it was a loaf of bread. 'Good heavens!' it cried. 'I've been reaped!'

Brandish: another word for a cereal bowl.

The multi-part comic-strip stories which appear on boxes of cornflakes are nothing more than breakfast serials!

An Italian restaurant can be judged by its pasta performance.

An excited American radio announcer once tried to urge his audience to 'get the best in bread'. Unfortunately, he didn't quite get the words right.

The reproof of the pudding is in the repeating.

Yesterday was Father's birthday, so Mother made Himalaya cake.

The wife of a distinguished classical scholar planned a special birthday cake for him. It was carefully decorated with quotations from the Greek poets. Unfortunately, it tasted awful. Thereby proving that we can't have archaic and eat it, too.

Is humble pie
Appease pudding?

She was a very confused bride. She found that she had put all her eggs in one biscuit.

'We have a new cuckoo makes nice tarts.'

As the pancake said to the syrup, 'You're so sweet, you should be in pitchers.'

Easter diet: ovoid chocolate!

If his new secretary
Isn't sweet in the daytime
And a little tart at night,
He'll saccharin the morning!

The cook wanted to serve horsemeat, but she couldn't stirrup any interest.

As any lover of shish kebabs knows, a sword can be used for duel purposes.

If you have decided to prepare Indian food for your guests, you must have the curries of your convictions.

A famous newspaper columnist, dining in a very expensive French restaurant in Mayfair, raved over the Trout Marguery. He summoned the proprietor of the restaurant and said, 'I'd like to have the recipe for this dish.' The proprietor smiled and answered quite suavely, 'I'm sorry, m'sieu, but we have the same policy here as you journalists. We never reveal our sauces.'

According to the native, 'Debate is what lures de fish!'

Tarzan went out to get the evening meal, but all he could catch was a couple of small birds and two baby chimpanzees. When Jane saw what he had brought home, she sighed, 'Not finch and chimps again!'

'Good Heavens! Cannibals!'
'Now, now, let's not get in a stew!'

What did the cannibal say after he had eaten his mother-in-law for dinner?
Gladiator.

Did you hear about the cannibalistic Arabs who were sitting under a palm tree eating their dates?

A couple with a mutual craving for something sweet drove to an ice-cream shop. Having bought ice-cream cones, they returned to the car to be comfortable. As they settled back to enjoy them, two birds landed on the car and began to chirp and flutter and peck at the windscreen. The husband finally figured out what they wanted. He opened his window and put his cone on the bonnet, whereupon the birds settled down to eat it. 'You're wonderful, George,' complimented his wife. 'How on earth did you think of that?' 'It was nothing,' he replied modestly. 'It was just a case of stilling two birds with one's cone!'

A harassed husband in Manchester hit his wife with a bowl of jelly. She emerged messy but unscathed. The husband was subsequently arrested for carrying a congealed weapon.

Said one strawberry to another: 'If we hadn't been in the same bed together last night, we wouldn't be in this jam now!'

Advice to young men: one should be cherry of virgins.

When Adam ate the fruit and fell from grace, it was a case of cores and defect.

'Shall we have a salad?' 'Yes, lettuce.'

Lovers' pledge: 'Lettuce forget those leeks of gossip and beetroot to each other.'

'Excuse me,' said Basil to Rosemary sagely, 'do you have the thyme?'

'Do you like a novel to be spicy?'
'It does nutmeg much difference.'

'Cinnamon' is a Scots colloquialism. For example, Old Mac-Intosh is a tightwad. When it comes to money, I've never cinnamon like him.

'Don't forget to add Worcester sauce,' she said with relish.

'May I have some consecrated lye?'

'You mean concentrated lye.'

'It does nutmeg much difference. That's what I camphor. What does it sulphur?'

'For 50 scents. I never cinnamon with so much wit!'

'Oh, ammonia novice. Thank you very much for the condiment!'

Absinthe is a French aphrodisiac. Hence the saying, 'Absinthe makes the tart grow fonder.'

There's a new kind of gum for people who simply detest the brands already on the market. It's called eschewing gum.

His wife bought a carpet in mint condition: it had a hole in the middle!

'I saw a big rat in my oven, but when I went for my gun, he ran out.'

'Did you shoot him?'

'No, he was out of my range!'

After all this food, how about something liquid?

'Water, water everywhere – but not a drop to drink.' 'Yes, I know. Water we going to do?'

When the naiad brought the god his drink, he nectar.

Patients convalescing at Mercy Hospital in Sydney, Australia, are served a brew named after a local bar. It is a rather lumpy beverage. However, this is because the koala tea of Mercy is not strained.

We like to sip Chinese tea slowly, but samovar friends prefer Russian.

'I thought you were staying for dinner.'
'No, I just camphor tea.'

And then there was the traveller on a liquid diet who went round the world in a tea daze!

'Waiter, this coffee tastes like mud!'
'That's strange, sir, it was fresh ground this morning!'

Recently seen advertisement: 'Milk. Nature in a glass by itself.'

Mrs White decided that she wanted to take a milk bath, so asked the milkman for fifty gallons of milk. 'Do you want it pasteurized?' asked the milkman. 'No,' she replied, 'up to my knees will be fine!'

When it comes to babies drinking milk, a little nipple do.

'Our baby is learning to talk!'
'What was the first thing he said, then?'
'Well, the other morning he woke up and asked me 'What's teat?'

Since he found a whey to make money, he's been doing much butter.

THIRST COME, THIRST SERVED

Candy is dandy, but liquor is quicker, wrote Ogden Nash, a man perfectly capable of rhyming *Jupiter* with *stupider* even while he was sober. Over to the world of alcohol: bars, pubs, wines, beer, and spirits . . .

As the unpopular wrestler said, 'I'm only here for the boos!'

When I'm stoned, I get a little boulder.

Famous wartime drinking song: 'Echelon Way to Tipperary'.

Everyone hates to see a grown man dry.

'Well!' exclaimed the wife. 'I hear that all those drinks you had at the club today didn't agree with you.' 'How did you hear that?' demanded the husband indignantly. 'Oh,' said the wife darkly, 'A little burp told me!'

Is a catnip a quick catatonic?

People pour mixed drinks soda party will last.

'I'm so thirsty that I could drink the Severn up.'

'And I'm so thirsty that I could drink Canada dry!'

The reformed alcoholic who falls from grace probably feels that he might as well relapse and enjoy it.

As the drunk in the hotel corridor said, '2B or not 2B?'

Mrs Elkie Hall swept out of the plush hotel and was almost upended by a tipsy pedestrian. The man started to apologize, but she froze him with a stare and muttered 'How gauche!' 'Just fine, lady,' answered the pedestrian, adding solicitously, 'and how gauche it with you?'

These days, people who drink before they drive are putting the quart before the hearse.

I've heard that a wunderbar is a great place for a drink.

A tied pub is presumably a trussed house?

A pub is the only place where you say cheers when they greet you with boos.

If bar drinks go metric, I hope it's schooner rather than litre!

When he's plastered,
He's a bundle of laths.

She'll do anything for a song or a drink,
So we offered a roundelay.

Anyone for a glass of wine?
Wine earth not?

The committee that runs one of the large claret-producing companies is known as the Bordeaux governors.

Champagne is just a false suffering.

My poodle loves good French wine. In fact, as I always say, give a dog a Beaune.

With a glass of whine,
You can have a wail of a time
Until the bawl is over!

Schnapps and hock are my favourite Teutonics.

There is a red Australian wine currently being marketed in London by a large chain of wine stores which goes by the name of Kanga Rouge!

Despite a violent downpour, the speaker managed to arrive at a banquet only an hour or so late. He was promptly served a glass of extremely bad wine. Downing it with some distaste, he sighed and muttered, 'Oh, well, any port in a storm!'

British Rail are currently running train excursions to different parts of the country which are well-known for their real ale. They are called Rail Ale excursions.

If the Chancellor of the Exchequer keeps on putting prices up, it'll be like a return to the old days. There'll be 21 shillings in a Guinness.

Here's to a stout end
To bitter days.
Ale's well that ends well.

Recipe for a slow-growing lawn: plant the seed deep and then soak with beer. The grass will eventually come up half cut.

Swedish beer: two pints make one cavort.

The disposable bottle has brought the beverage industry to the pint of no return.

Widespread advertisement for lager: 'Keep taking the Pils.'

A drunk staggered into a funeral parlour and demanded a Scotch and soda. When the undertaker explained where he was, the drunk pulled himself together and announced with dignity, 'Well, sir, in that case, you may give me a bier.'

'What is't? A spirit?' William Shakespeare

He tells jokes only when he's drunk. He has a rye sense of humour.

Amorous male: 'How about coming over to my place for a whisky and soda?'
Cautious female: 'Well, you could talk me into a gin and platonic!'

Tequila is known as the gulp of Mexico.

Charged with trying to push his girlfriend out of a window, the Mexican protested, 'We were just dancing. I wasn't trying tequila!'

Could you add anything to this dialogue even if you wanted to?
Girl: 'Leave me beer I'll scream.'
Boy: 'I'd like tequila! I didn't ask gin!'
Girl:'Water you mean? Then wine you let me go? Orange juice sorry you hurt me?'
Boy: 'Don't be soda pressed. Them martini bruises.'
Girl: 'Oh, why Chianti leave me alone?'
Boy: 'Look, vodka I do to make everything all rye?'
Girl: 'Well, we could give up this bourbon life. There's more rum to fight in the country!'

In lighter vein (cigarettes, of course):
I've heard that cigarettes can lead to coughin'.

Cigarette life if you don't weaken.

Smoking is the hot tip
That's a dead cert.

Said the punter, 'I had a hot tip on a horse called Cigarette, but I didn't have enough tobaccer!'

Did you hear about the cigarette smoker who went insane and ended up in a menthol hospital?

To refuse a cigarette, just say, 'No tar.'

He tried to make me smoke, but I said I'd see him inhale first.

I'd blow smoking tomorrow if it wasn't such a fag!

As one homosexual said to another, 'Have a fag.'

There were three men in a boat with four cigarettes but no matches. What did they do? They threw out one cigarette, and that made the boat a cigarette lighter!

'I hate cigarette smoking. It can be such a drag!'

He likes to smoke menthol cigarettes and enjoy a drink at the same time. You could say he was into mentholated spirits!

'Grass' is a term that reefers to marijuana.

I went to this drug party and all that the guests could say was 'High!'

All modern-day novels have their heroin.

Taking drugs is just another way of going to pot.

11

ITALIAN LEPIDOPTERIST FINDS ROME ANTS

If love were all . . .

'You aren't as gallant as when you were a boy,' pouted the wife. 'No,' admitted the husband, 'and you aren't as buoyant as when you were a gal!'

'I'm afraid my poor wife can never have a child,' sighed a frustrated husband. 'Inconceivable!' commented a friend. 'No, unbearable,' said the husband. 'Impregnable,' amended the friend.

'Whenever I come home on payday, my wife says, "Glad to see you, handsome!" '
'Handsome?'
'Yes, hand some over!'

Her husband spent a large part of the party staring at another woman. The wife finally turned to him and said, 'May I have the next glance, please?'

'My husband is a great lover; he knows all the erroneous zones!'

When the blonde he married turned into a brunette, he sued for bleach of promise.

After another woman had turned his head, he couldn't face his wife.

At first, she seemed to be his dream come true, but in the end he decided that she was really just a passing fiancée.

A wolf is a man who treats all women as sequels.

It's better to have loved a short girl than never to have loved a tall.

The Eskimo approach when trying to pick up a girl: 'What's an ice girl like you doing in a place like this?'

'I've just had a letter from my daughter. She's in love with a dozen soldiers. But she says not to worry; it's all very platoonic.'

Why is a lovely young lady like a hinge?
She is something to adore, especially if she is a swinger.

She put her arms around me, squeezed and said, 'This is my only vice.'

Courtship is when you try each other for sighs.

'I chose this cliff to propose because I love view.'

'Will you marry me?'
'No, I'm afraid not.'
'Oh, come on, be a support!'

The organist was instrumental in our marriage.

Some tie marriage knots with gold,
While others prefer platinum.

'Your wife never stops talking. How on earth can you stand it?' marvelled a henpecked husband's best friend. 'I know,' sighed the husband, 'I've given that woman the best ears of my life.'

His marriage is on the rocks – but things may improve when they get a bed.

Gossip column reporter to film star: 'Is it true that your new bride has been married five times and that you have been married just twice?' The star's reply: 'Yes, she's three chumps ahead of me!'

I dislike you some days,
But love unites.

The latest sex manual is all-embracing.

Sign on the gate of a nudist colony: 'Come in. We are never clothed.'

There is a world copulation explosion.

When the masochist married, he admitted that it was love at first slight.

Sex has its pros and cons. The pros get arrested, and the cons get married.

Monogamy leaves a lot to be desired.

Advice given to boys: 'If at first you don't succeed, try a little ardour.'

12

WHOSE GAME?

Games, pastimes, hobbies – anything, in fact, at which people like to work harder than they do at work. These are games you sit down for . . .

Chinese checkers is just another game for Oriental grocery clerks.

With games like Scrabble and Monopoly, you get board.

'I will have one last game of bridge, and then Go,' said the games fanatic.

'I never seem to get a hand with jacks, queens and kings,' she said tenaciously.

Is it true that pontoon is a form of bridge?

Last knight, a bishop was rooked by a queen selling pawn in the King's Road.

He always gets poor cards – you have to hand it to him.

'I'd love a game of draughts,' he said airily.

'I've heard that there are clubs for spades who give girls diamonds to win their hearts.'

I said, 'Why don't we sit a little closer? After all, it is contact bridge!'

... and games you can't sit down for ...

Said the male jogger to the female jogger: 'My pace or yours?'

'Sure I'd like a swim. Can you wade for a minute?'

'I like to watch a game of tennis in silence, but there's usually too much racquet going on.'

Three young ladies were seated in a West End pub. One was called to the phone and was overheard to say, 'Fine! I'll see you there about eightish!' A few minutes later, the second girl was called to the phone. 'Nineish? That'll be great!' she said Left alone, the third girl sighed and stood up. Turning to the men at the bar, she called, 'Tennish, anyone?'

Cricketer's motto: 'You're only as young as you field.'

In hockey, it's the net result that counts.

During an international basketball tournament, the countries with very tall players were running away with all the matches. Observed a spectator, 'Many lands make height work!'

'I get a kick out of football,' he said gamely.

You need leather balls to play rugby.

A skiing match can be a slalom occasion.

It's been said that wrestling is the sport of clings.

Weight-lifting is a hard way to hernia living.

Though he worked hard teaching me the art of rowing, he never got it into my scull.

Sailing is a crewed business.

'Do you like cycling with a group?' 'No, doing things in groups gets the wind up me. I prefer to cyclone!'

A group of brave souls were having their first lesson in sky-diving. 'What if the parachute doesn't open?' asked one, meekly. 'That,' said the instructor grimly, 'is what we call jumping to a conclusion.'

'Your horses always come in last,' she nagged.

A fishing trip is a reel treat.

Madder music, stronger wine, and more terrible puns . . .
Flamenco dancing is a Stamp Act.

Folk dancing is making hey while the moon shines.

Traditional ballroom dancing is really a form of floorplay.

Ballroom dancing is sometimes referred to as a navel engagement.

Now that we're in the Common Market, is there any room for a Belgian conga?

She never liked going to dances; she was a waltzflower.

She has a flare for the piano. You can see by her Very light touch.

Banging together brass plates in an orchestra isn't as cymbal as it looks.

To do a tapestry, you needle the wool you can get.

Trick photography is a lot of focus-pocus.

An eight-year-old lad was a persistent and dedicated collector of postage stamps, until the kid next door bought an album and started a collection, too. 'Clarence buys every stamp I do,' complained the eight-year-old to his father. 'He's taken all the fun out of it for me. I'm packing up!' 'Don't be a fool, lad,' counselled his father. 'Remember the old saying: Imitation is the sincerest form of philately.'

The secretary of the local Women's Institute group asked the members how many would be interested in a course in glove-making. They all looked a little embarrassed. Finally, one woman said she thought they all knew as much as they needed to know from watching people do it in the cinema and on television.

The trouble with gardening is that it's a yard life.

The travelling vaudeville show in the late nineteenth and early twentieth centuries was often a tour de farce.

'Banshee' is a sort of stag party.

The purpose of New Year's Eve is to give parents some relief from the Christmas holly daze.

The trouble with society today is that in winter people are forsaking the great outdoors for the grate indoors.

13

SOMETHING FOR EVERY BODY

The nose is in the middle of your face because it's the scenter.

'Have your eyes ever been checked?'
'No, they've always been brown!'

Her jokes are like her eyes; blue as the sea, only cornea.

A student returned to college after spending a weekend at Lulworth Cove. He had a black eye and a badly swollen lip. 'Run into a door?' a friend inquired. 'No,' replied the adventurer ruefully, 'I was struck by the beauty of the place!'

A man was concerned over whether his new electric toothbrush would injure the enamel on his teeth. His worries were unfounded when he discovered that the tooth is stronger than friction.

'My brother and I both hate to wash behind arrears.'

Baldness is a kind of failure. Wish I'd made the greyed.

The bald facts: hair today, gone tomorrow.

Many years ago, when men still lived in caves, baldness was unhaired of.

'Those are the bald facts,' he said smoothly.

The wig-maker asked him how he wanted toupée his bill.

'Yul be sorry,' he bawled at her.

I told the solitary pedestrian that he had B.O. And he replied, 'That's why I wore cologne.'

'Did you hear about the two blood cells?'
'No, what happened?'
'They loved in vein.'

I Euston know the main-line stations: St Pancreas, Victorear, Padding-tum, Liverpool Street, Marrowly-bone, and Chair-ing Cross.

Puberty is a hair-raising experience.

Adolescence is the stage between puberty and adultery.

'Don't hit me in the bellicose it hurts.'

Astronomer to offended female assistant: 'All I said was, "I can see Uranus quite clearly tonight!"'

Little is known about the salivary glands because they are so secretive.

'I must have damaged my glands when I fell over yesterday. I've got this dreadful lymph.'

When people casually dismiss a female's tantrums and say it's her glands, do they really mean she's a lymphomaniac?

Old age is when your heir apparent becomes a parent.

Ladies' room graffiti: Lay off the Pill and let nature take its curse.

The secret of being a happy woman over forty is not to worry about the menopause but the men who don't.

Well-known song: 'Thanks for the Mammary.'

Old men in burlesque houses are just wandering down mammary lane.

The brain is nothing more than a memory gland.

Is a penal colony an all-male nudist camp?

Would a male contraceptive pill make such a vas deferens?

Going to bed with some people can lead to a foetal error.

The best position for sleeping is curled up. Anyway, your foetal feel better.

Women take fertility drugs because of a misconception.

Said a newspaper report: 'The report said that the drugs might cause girth defects if administered to pregnant women.'

As the queen said to her king, 'Darling, I think I'm regnant.'

My mother was a labour organizer in a maternity ward. She always said, 'Those scabs will go away if you don't picket them.'

Said the perplexed Oriental father, 'Our new baby son is very white!' Replied his wife defensively, 'Well, Occidents do happen!'

Is a pas de deux a father of twins?

'I've got eighteen kids,' she said overbearingly.

'There is no cure for this disease.' *Hilaire Belloc*
   TB or not TB, that is the congestion.

'Basic' is a word meaning upset by ground swell.

The gymnast who fell off the parallel bars had a tough break: he was parallelized!

I've had this cough for exactly seven days. My doctor says it's just a wee cold.

I got up this morning not feeling too well, so I decided to have a wee cough.

He opened the door and influenza.

Inquired St Peter of the latest arrival, 'And how did you get here?' Came the reply, 'Flu!'

Please excuse
Ym shguoc dna sezeens
But I've got this terrible code.

Sneezing is much achoo about nothing.

In the winter, it's hard to keep warm if you have a bad coal.

When a liar gets pharyngitis, he loses his vice.

'Why had Eve no fear of measles?'
'Because she'd Adam.'

'I have a bad heart,' he murmured.

Is a hospital consultant who specializes in hearts an auricle oracle?

I've heard that epilepsy is really the survival of the fit.

VD is nothing to clap about.

When the glassblower inhaled, he got a pane in his stomach.

A funny accident can leave you in stitches.

An explorer in Africa fell sick and summoned a witch doctor, who examined him carefully, and then presented him with a leather thong. 'Bite off an inch of this thong every day,' he prescribed. 'Chew it carefully and at the end of a week, you'll be as good as new.' When he returned a week later, though, the witch doctor found the explorer sicker than ever. The witch doctor demanded, 'How come?' The explorer replied weakly, 'The thong is ended, but the malady lingers on.'

Being castrated is a eunuch experience.

Some women have their breasts inflated with silicone so that they can join the jut set.

'I've just had a very serious operation,' he said half-heartedly.

Did you hear about the cardiologist who always operated on his patients at the foot of a large chimney? He was a grate believer in open hearth surgery!

'I twisted my ankle,' he said limply.
'Does that mean you have a fracture?' she asked brokenly.

The theatre of operations . . .
    Is a gynaecologist's office a cervix station?

Many people are in favour of phasing pain beds out of the National Health Service.

In Ireland, there's a National Elf Service.

He thought his life was coming to a full stop. But thanks to his surgeon, it only came to a semi-colon.

When he said he was a sturgeon, I knew there was something fishy about him.

To qualify for work in a hospital, you must learn to do things in an orderly fashion.

Motto of the London Ambulance Service: Sic Transit.

A clerk recently had to be committed to a mental hospital. Every time he went into a pub, he kept hearing strange invoices.

A lady in a hospital, recovering from a minor operation, was awakened from a nap by a knock on the door. 'Who goes there?' she inquired warily. 'Friend or enema?'

'I'm at your cervix,' said the gynaecologist.
'Dilated to meet you,' replied his patient.

The doctor was examining a pretty young girl who had a chest cold. 'Now then,' he said, raising his stethoscope, 'big breaths!' 'Yeth, thir,' she replied proudly, 'and I'm only thixteen!'

To be successful, a doctor must have a lot of patience.

Some doctors practise acupuncture in order to pick up pin money. (Talking of acupuncture, some of its tools are believed by some to be cure awls.)

'Doctor, will I be given a general or local anaesthetic?' 'You can have ether.'

The only way a medicine man can keep fit is to exorcise.

When the missionary fell sick in darkest Africa, he was asked witch doctor he would like to see.

The surgeon decided to take a day off work to enjoy the sunshine. Unfortunately, he was found out and doctor day's pay!

A kindly doctor assures every patient, 'This injection won't hurt a bit.' Unfortunately for the patient, that's an M.D. promise.

Lawyer: 'Did you say the plaintiff was shot in the woods, doctor?'
Doctor: 'I did not. I said he was shot in the lumbar region!'

The guru refused to let his dentist freeze his jaw because he wanted to transcend dental medication.

The doctor had to let his nurse go because she kept needling all his patients.

'It's time for your jab,' injected the nurse.

His nurse became very friendly when his pay cheque cauterize.

Nature's warning to slow down . . .
   It isn't the cough
   That carries you off,
   It's the coffin,
   They carry you off in.

It was ironic that after passing seven exams in common law he died intestate.

An American tourist in London was confused by traffic driving on the 'wrong' side of the road. Before too long, he was run over. He regained consciousness in a casualty ward and moaned, 'Did I come here to die?' 'Oh, no, sir,' the cockney nurse assured him, 'you came here yesterdie!'

Coroner: this is what death is just around.

When you breathe, you inspire.
When you don't, you expire.

An undertaker was sliding a coffin into his hearse on a cold winter's day when it slipped out of his hands, landed on the ice-covered pavement, skidded down a hill, went through the open door of a chemist's shop, and slid past the shop's prescription counter. The undertaker was chasing along after the coffin, puffing and wheezing. As he got to the prescription counter, he said to the pharmacist there, 'For heaven's sake, give me something to stop this coffin!'

Sign seen outside an East London cemetery: 'Due to manpower shortages, graves will be dug by our skeleton staff.'

Good jokes never die: they only pass along. For example, the comedian's wife sued for divorce, claiming that he tried to joke her to death.

'I'm dying,' he croaked.

14

WHO'S HADYN MY CHOPIN LIZST?

Epunymous characters . . .

Printed on the wall over a loo in a London pub is the mis-spelled request 'Please wiggel Handel.' Below it, some music-lover has scrawled, 'If I do, will it wiggel Bach?'

Is Haydn seek a hunt for a long-lost musical score?

Smetana showed up by mistake one night at a theatre across the street from the one in which his opera *The Bartered Bride* was playing. The problem was that he didn't know which side his bride was bartered on.

He claims the footprint is that of the Abominable Snowman, Yeti's evidence is pretty spoorious.

The first pun ever made is credited, logically enough, to Adam. Eve teased him, 'What's wrong with eating this little old apple?' Adam answered, 'I'll bite.' The next day, they both had to give up Eden.

How were Adam and Eve kept from gambling?
Their pair o'dice was taken away from them.

When Eve tried to get out of the garden without him, Adam called up to the Commanding Officer, 'Eve is absent without leaf!'

'I wonder what Eve is going to bring for dinner,' said Adam fruitlessly.

While we all have our foibles, Aesop became famous for his.

Alice had a very bad temper for a little girl. That's why she threw the looking-glass.

At the height of the Watergate scandal in Washington, New York Times journalist James Reston predicted that a book would eventually be written about the whole affair – called *Malice in Blunderland*.

When Archimedes had his bright idea in the bath, he jumped out and ran down the street just as he was, yelling, 'Eureka! Eureka!' The policeman standing on the street corner asked, 'Eureka what?' Beginning to feel a little foolish, Archimedes replied, 'Eureka garlic. Yes, that's it, eureka garlic!'

On the first day that she met him, Lady Guinevere asked King Arthur, 'Arthur any more at home like you?'

When Zeus banished him to Africa to uphold the heavens, his faithful girlfriend went with him sighing, 'Atlas, we are alone!'

Thomas à Becket built a fireplace in his outside loo, and thus had a can for all seasons.

Jack Benny's insistence on always being thirty-nine proved that he was good in comedy but badinage.

On his first visit to England, an ambitious American tried to gatecrash a garden party at Buckingham Palace, but was kicked out. Picking himself up from the ground, he observed gingerly, 'Evidently Britannia will not waive the rules!'

Did Julius Caesar with decorum in the forum?

Needless to say, the Vatican isn't inclined to believe infidel Castro.

Detective Charlie Chan was once assigned to discover who was stealing the cargoes of tea that were being shipped in from the Orient. Consequently, he became America's first China tea cop.

Lady Chatterley loved her gardener, even though he was a little bit too rough around the hedges.

The young student of literature was dawdling over his third cup of coffee at the breakfast table one Sunday morning while reading *The Canterbury Tales*. 'What have you got there?' his father inquired casually. 'Oh,' answered the lad, 'just my cup and Chaucer.'

Chauvinism is bellicose patriotism, and occurs in phrases such as 'Who are you chauvin?' and 'Watch who you're chauvin.'

Every time the handsome young prince found a girl that he thought might be Cinderella, he went down to defeat.

Cleopatra was the queen of denial.

What Cleopatra really whispered to Mark Antony when he asked her if she was true to him was 'Omar Khayyam!'

Cleopatra instituted the practice of keeping a handkerchief tucked in her cleavage, and thus became famous for taking a wiper to her bosom.

When Antony saw how Cleopatra handled snakes, he certainly made an asp of himself.

Oh, I should like to see Columbus's birthplace,
And then I'd write a fine authentic poem,
And critics, none of whom would read it through,
Would say, 'At last we have the Genoan article!'

When Columbus sailed across the Atlantic and back without taking a bath, the Queen of Spain called him a dirty double crosser.

An Egyptian led his party into Cairo's largest mosque and announced, 'Here the sons of our great leader Nasser and his friends learned to worship God and his prophet Mohammed.' But a Maoist from Shanghai interrupted from the edge of the crowd, 'That's not the way my Chinese ancestors tell it.' The guide looked pained and remarked, 'Just a minute, everyone. There seems to be a little Confucian around here!'

Noël Coward: a husband afraid to come home from the office's Christmas party.

Robinson Crusoe originated the four-day week; he had all his work done by Friday.

Cupid's aim is pretty good, but he still makes a lot of Mrs.

As a tribute to their great leader, the French are planning to take over the Rock of Gibraltar and rename it de Gaulle Stone.

In the 1950s news photos, President Eisenhower and Mr Krushchev always stood out in bald contrast.

When Queen Elizabeth 1 made a state visit to the City of London, the Lord Mayor greeted her with, 'Hail to the Queen!' Her Majesty stared at him. 'How dare you hail,' she demanded angrily, 'while I am reigning!'

A Valentine: My heart and I call to you,
          But you're too deaf to Eros.

Eve was just a rib-off.

When it came to drinking, comedian W. C. Fields was a veteran who suffered from bottle fatigue.

I heard that Baron Frankenstein was a lonely man until he discovered how to make friends.

The liberal MP Clement Freud is a well-known cook. He introduced Freud eggs to this country.

'That's a very Freudian remark,' she said dreamily.

As his biographer said to George Gershwin, 'Let us beguine at the beginning.'

'Arse' is a Middle English variant spelling or 'horse'. Hence, Lady Godiva rode through town on her . . .

Lorne Green, who used to play Ben Cartwright in the television series *Bonanza*, was well-known for his deep bass voice. One day, he was trying to make a long-distance telephone call with the help of the operator. She asked him if he had the code. 'No,' rumbled the actor, 'I talk this way all the time.'

'Enough of your fairy tales,' he said Grimmly.

The famous Stripper Gypsy Rose Lee woke up one morning and found herself fully dressed. 'Good heavens!' she gasped, 'I've been draped!'

Keir Hardie was responsible for the birth of the Labour Party.

Oliver Wendell Holmes was a physician as well as an author and lecturer. He is said to have remarked of his medical career that he was grateful for small fevers.

Sherlock Holmes was always photographed in street attire. He was a cloak and daguerreotype.

In 1977, a satirical version of some of the adventures of Sherlock Holmes was shown on television. A frequent remark made by Holmes to his intimate friend and recorder of his adventures, Watson, is 'Elementary, my dear Watson!' In the television version of Holmes's adventures, there was a lovely scene where Watson was attempting to solve a newspaper crossword. The answers were beyond Watson, so he kept reading out the clues to Holmes. Holmes managed to solve the clues in a most amusing way, as illustrated by these four clues and answers:

'A large plant having a woody trunk and bearing citrus fruit (1,5,4)'
'A lemon tree, my dear Watson!'
'In the manner of a certain city in western California (1,2,8)'
'A la Monterey, my dear Watson!'
'A Conservative politician paying an allowance for supporting his wife after their divorce (7,4)'
'Alimony Tory, my dear Watson!'
'A pale-yellow-coloured flat-bodied fish (1,5,5,3)'
'A lemon manta ray, my dear Watson!'

To complement the four examples above, here are another four sets of clues to answers:

'Type of canal(10)'
'Alimentary, my dear Watson!'
'Enlightening (12)'
'Illuminatory, my dear Watson!'
'A door made from a soft yellowish resin that comes from tropical trees (5,5)'
'Elemi entry, my dear Watson!'

'A type of citrus concoction served between main courses of a dinner (1,5,6)'
'A lemon entrée, my dear Watson!'

* * * *

Robin Hood was just a hood robbin' the rich to pay the poor.

'Accidents will happen,' said Captain Hook off-handedly.

A friend once asked Ben Jonson to make a pun. He replied, 'Pun what subject?' His friend thought for a moment, and said, 'Why not the King?' 'But,' said Jonson, 'the King is not a subject. He is the King!'

When it was first published, one reviewer wrote of *Finnegans Wake*: 'Last night I chose to read a new book. It turned out to be an unfortunate Joyce.'

Question seen on lots of old postcards: 'Do you like Kipling?'
Answer: 'I don't know. I've never kippled!'

The plantation owners were appalled when President Abraham Lincoln decided to freedom slaves.

There's a finance company in one of the western states of USA called 'The Loan Arranger'.

At the court of Versailles, King Louis XV noticed during a reception that one of Madame de Pompadour's petticoats was showing. 'My sweet,' he informed her gallantly, 'your quelque shows!'

King Louis XV's royal barge capsized one day while on the Seine. When Madame de Pompadour heard this news, she asked if her precious kitten had been saved. Unfortunately, Louis had to tell her, 'Un, deux, trois cats sank.'

Molly Malone used to wheel her wheelbarrow through streets broad and narrow. It soon became apparent to her customers that she was a shellfish girl.

The signatures of uneducated cowboys who ride the plains of South America are known as gaucho marks.

A piece of dialogue from an old Marx Brothers' film: 'What has four legs and a trunk?' 'That's irrelevant!' 'That's-a-right, irrelevant!'

According to the writer H. L. Mencken, two housewives arguing across their back porches can never agree because they are arguing from different premises.

King Midas had a gilt complex.

I told him that I liked his pictures, but I didn't think they were worth the Monet.

The Moses film project was abandoned after they'd seen the rushes.

Mozart always wanted to get ahead; he was an opera-tunist!

Senator Edmund Muskie was a candidate for the Presidency of the USA in 1972, but was beaten by Richard Nixon. This is a reported story about Senator Muskie. He was on a goodwill tour of the Middle East, and was about to enter a Cairo mosque. One of his aides demurred about following the Islamic custom of removing shoes before entering a mosque. The aide explained that he had a hole in one of his socks. Muskie shrugged it off. 'After all,' he said, 'we are in a holy place!'

As Naomi admitted, 'Ruth is stranger than fiction!'

Teacher: 'Johnnie, can you tell the class what nationality Napoleon was?'
Johnnie: 'Course I can!'
Teacher: 'That's right.'

Famous men have different skeletal structures from other people. This can be proved by the fact that Napoleon was a Bonaparte.

Neptune is seeking.

Richard Nixon was elected President of the United States in November 1968. The morning after the election, his daughter Julie presented him with a Presidential Seal that she had stitched and framed. Mr Nixon later described it as 'the kindest thing that I had happen, even though it's crewel.'

After being subjected to numerous speeches of welcome, Prince Philip is alleged to have remarked, 'It never wanes but it bores!'

The generosity of Sir Cecil Rhodes has enabled thousands of students to see the world through Rhodes Scholared glasses.

Sax Rohmer once threatened to write a sequel to his series of novels on the villain Fu-Manchu. He was going to call it *Many Men Smoke but Fu-Manchu.*

The Marquis de Sade never invited anyone for dinner. His friends just dropped in for smacks.

Samson loved Delilah, until she bald him out.

Is Santa Claus a beatnik on the day after Christmas?

Beware of Satan or evil have his way.

Shakespeare was so busy writing plays that he never had time to shave. That's why he was known as the Beard of Avon.

One hot day in spring, Shakespeare decided to desist from writing sonnets to his Anne and take her for a swim at a nearby beach. They had to don their swimsuits from the previous year, and it suddenly occurred to Will that moths had quite likely been feeding on his trunks. 'Wouldst thou investigate, my love?' he asked his companion. She made a thorough but discreet examination, and then cheerfully reported, 'No holes, Bard!'

If they asked me what Shakespeare called the Globe, I'd politely say 'A wooden O.'

The phrase 'George Bernard Shaw was born in Island' is both a littoral mistake and a printer's Eire. (Are you sure?)

The famous Dr Spooner called on the Dean of Christ Church, and inquired, 'Is the bean dizzy?'

Speaking to a group of farmers, Spooner reportedly said, 'I have never before addressed so many tons of soil.' (What on earth made him say that? It wasn't at all humus.)

Spooner was visiting a friend at his new country cottage: Complimented the Doctor, 'It's a nosey little cook you have here!'

As St Peter says to every new arrival as they approach the Pearly Gates, 'Well, halo there!'

Tarzan is just the short name for the American flag. Its full name is the Tarzan Stripes.

Going through the woods one day, a man came across a boy with an apple on his head and a stopwatch in his hand. 'What are you trying to do?' inquired the man. Without moving his head, and still looking straight ahead, the boy answered out of the side of his mouth, 'Time Will Tell.' (Did the lad have an arrow escape?)

The little boy was counting on his Uncle Alf to take him to the circus which was in town. On the big day, though, the lad's mum told him that Uncle Alf had flown to Australia to watch the Davis Cup tennis matches. 'I didn't even know he liked tennis,' complained the lad. 'Oh, but he does,' his mum assured him. 'Indeed, many's the time I've heard Alfred laud tennis, son!'

The Scandinavian god introduced himself to the pretty young goddess. 'I am Thor,' he rumbled.
To which she replied, 'Well, come up and thee me when you feel better, then!'

The three Musketeers were pretty fency fellows.

A tourist purchased an old painting while he was on holiday in Italy. When he arrived home in London, he took it to a leading dealer to get his opinion of its worth. 'Well,' said the dealer tactfully, 'I'd say it is either a Titian or a repetition.'

Toulouse-Lautrec, the famous French painter, was once invited home by a *demi-mondaine* who teased him, 'What have you got, Toulouse?'

When Canada's Prime Minister, Pierre Trudeau, appeared to have mouthed an expletive in Parliament, it was reported that he prefers to be obscene and not heard!

Oliver Twist wasn't a bad lad, but someone was always urchin him on.

The pun in the title of the play *The Importance of Being Earnest* was a Wilde idea!

Brigham Young was explaining to an overseas journalist his reasons for having so many wives. 'But,' interrupted the journalist, 'M'sieu, that is rather a wonderful thing you have done, to have married so many!' 'Yes,' conceded Young, 'it is bigamy!'

'Carmen' is a term commonly used by cooks. It commonly occurs in the phrase 'Carmen get it.'

There was once a little girl named Carmen Cohen. Her mother always called her Carmen, but her father, for obscure reasons, always hailed her as Cohen. As a result of this, by the time the girl had reached her teens, she just didn't know whether she was Carmen or Cohen.

What did the boys all shout when they spotted attractive Cynthia as she walked up the street? 'Hiya Cynth!'

Once upon a time, after a trawler fisherman had gone to sea, his wife gave birth to twins. Aware that her husband seldom agreed with her decisions, yet needing a pair of names for the children, she turned to his brother for help. On his return, the fisherman, having admired his new son and daughter, asked his wife what she had named them. She confessed that she had let his brother choose the names. 'He called our darling daughter Denise,' she explained. 'Well, that's a pretty good choice,' admitted the father. 'And what did he call our son?' 'Oh,' his wife replied, 'he's Denephew!'

Dinah saw a large prehistoric animal!

If you should ever buy a female ass and have problems thinking of a suitable name for her, just remember this: Dolores, an ass!

A young Air Force cadet managed to get himself engaged to two attractive girls at one and the same time. One was called Edith, and the other was called Kate. Unfortunately for the cadet, the two girls met, discovered his two-timing ways, and confronted him, crying, 'You can't have your Kate and Edith, too!'

Said the rather tipsy girl, 'When I drink too much, Eileen to one side.'

Erminduke and Marmatrude are pen-friends. They've been exchanging letters for some time.

If a girl called Lisa wanted to introduce herself to a fellow called Gene at a party where all the guests had to dress like Tarzan or his girlfriend Jane, how would she go about such an introduction? 'Eugene, Melissa!'

'Drinking all this alcohol makes one Gideon dizzy,' muttered the inebriated youth.

After her divorce had finally come through, she said, 'I'm Gladys all over' in a matter-of-fact tone.

Did you hear about the atheist? He was Godfrey!

Henry the cannibal had a wife: Henrietta!

Señor Ringer, when asked about his wife, replied, 'My wife, Isabella Ringer.'

One day, Prince Jacques and his sister Jill went for a walk with the royal jester. Unfortunately, Jacques fell down and broke his clown, and Jill came tumbling after.

As the overfamiliar boy said to the inexperienced girl, 'Jemima asking your name?'

At a golf club in Mexico City, a member returned unexpectedly to his suite to find his wife in the arms of the club's manager, Señor Juan. The outraged husband promptly pulled out a revolver and shot the manager. The club's golf pro heard the shot and rushed into the room. Taking in the situation at a glance, he clapped the husband on the back and exclaimed, 'Well done, sir! At last someone round here has made a hole in Juan!'

'I try to keep everything nicely polished,' she sighed. 'I wish I could chamois like my sister Kate!'

Did you hear about the career girl who was always Jocelyn for position?

It's true that Spanish labourers are usually Manuel workers.

Advice given to a rather lazy girl: 'Marion, haste and repent at leisure!'

Maurice, a miner, was the bull-nosed fellow from Oxford.

As the husband said to his somewhat distracted wife, 'Ophelia not really listening to me.'

When asked to describe her husband, the wife said he was Solomon proper.

The Irish musician left the pub at eleven o'clock. He was Titus O'Drum.

15

TO ERR IS HUMOUR

This is the chapter where you will find all the worthwhile puns which don't fall neatly into the various other chapters and obviously couldn't be expunged . . .

When a couple of monocles get together and make spectacles of themselves, does it create glass distinction?

'Take that pencil out of your mouth, Timothy, and commonplace it on my desk.'

'Bidet' was once defined as D-Day minus two.

It's been said that the guillotine is a French chopping centre.

Flattery is . . . living in an apartment.

An igloo is . . . an icicle built for two.

Juice is . . the population of Israel.

A modern armchair is . . . a vinyl resting place.

Lynching is . . . trial by fury.

Aloof is . . . the top of a Chinese house.

The inventor of the front-door bell was of great assistance to the knock need.

The pupils were given a holiday while the school was closed for altercations.

Racial superiority is a pigment of your imagination.

Is a muddle a beautiful gull that poses in pitchers?

The Exorcist was both a book and a film about sorcery in which it quickly became apparent that possession is nine points of the lore.

Is a book on voyeurism called a peeping tome?

A fad is something that goes in one era and out the other.

A white lie is aversion of the truth.

A pacifist is a flag-waiver.

'Bigamist' is an Italian fog.

'Bigotry' is an Italian redwood.

An egotist is a person who suffers from I strain.

When he announced what he had in mind, it's what he sediment.

When is a door not a door? When it's a jar.

It was called 'The Fiddle Hotel' because it was such a vile inn.

'Dismal' is a method of counting invented on the Continent. For example, dismal currency, dismal arithmetic, dismal notation, and especially dismal places.

Spy novels are so thrilling that you want to read them from covert to covert!

An espionage chief urged his staff to cut down on long expensive telegrams. The order which he circulated to his staff read: 'Don't wire until you see the flights of their spies.'

He called me woodenhead
So I gave him a piece of my mind.
And now he's got a chip on his shoulder.

When asked how they were going to blow up the enemy ship, the leader of the explosives team replied, 'Your guess is as good as mine.'

Benign: is what you can't wait to be when you're eight.

Corporal punishment smacks of sadism.

'Give an example of period furniture.'
'The electric chair, because it ends a sentence.'

Since he didn't farewell, he left without further adieu!

Allegro is . . . a chorus line.

If you have to shovel the snow off your front path, you're infra dig.

Soupçon is French for a small amount,
Only morceau.

Coq d'or is . . . the entrance marked 'Gentlemen.'

The height of insignificance: being none in a million.

Every day is the dawn of a new error.

'What's a Greek urn?'
'About thirty drachmas a week.'

An ambitous North American Indian decorated his wigwam with all sorts of cheap and nasty baubles. His neighbour felt that the decorated wigwam was bringing down the whole tone of the neighbourhood. The ambitious Indian couldn't understand why the neighbour was less friendly than he once had been. When he tried to discuss this with the second Indian, the neighbour just pointed to the ambitious Indian's wigwam and grumbled, 'Cheap Sioux veneer.'

Do all Norwegians have a troll sense of humour?

We wanted to hear a little Indian music, but we couldn't find a baby sitar.

The old Christmas spirit is like artificial holly: dead and berried.

Christmas stockings are nothing more than childish hang-ups.

A famous writer once sent Christmas cards containing nothing but 25 different letters of the alphabet. When a few of his friends admitted to being somewhat perplexed, he pointed to the card and cried, 'Look! No L!'

He's highly strung and describes himself as self-taut. (That spelling is intensional.)

My children prefer to be punished in the heat of the moment, rather than waiting until I scold.

To win the status race, you need two loos.

I feel so strongly about loo graffiti that I've signed a partition.

The world's population explosion is caused by all the overbearing women.

'The only reason that I can suggest for my ex-boyfriend spreading such nasty rumours is that he has it infamy!'

'I've just seen a stage version of *The Female Eunuch*. The cast rating was superb!'

Because Fifi has a 39.37-inch bust,
Men love to metre.
But I just don't know what it is they see
In two decimal places.

If you're going to have a meeting of the sexes, take my advice – you need agenda.

'Even though you have a bad code, I still cipher you.'

Is someone who needs no introduction beyond compère?

She said I was the kind she could go for. But I wish I had been the kind she could stay for.

She's the May Queen; I hope to be May King!

A perfectionist was about to be shown a house in London's Belgravia. 'Here,' boasted the estate agent, 'is the house-owner's dream, a house without a flaw.' 'Without a flaw,' echoed the perfectionist. 'But what is one supposed to walk on?'

'I was neutral until a live wire promised me the earth.'

Why is coal the most contradictory article in the world of commerce?
Because, when it's been purchased, it goes to the cellar.

Having brought the house down,
He said he didn't know that it was liable to claps.
(Which seemed applausible storey.)

'What colours would you paint the sun and the wind?' 'Oh, let me see. I'd say the sun rose and the wind blue.'

An American shirt-maker, renowned for his garishness, offered rewards to people who could dream up new names for colours like 'dark blue', 'light brown', and so on. The names that he received included such items as 'forever amber', 'sick bay', 'unpredictible fuchsia', 'statutory grape', 'dorian grey', 'gang green', 'well red', and 'hi-yo silver'!

Overheard in a Chelsea pub: 'You could tell she was going to be fastidious. Her father was fast and her mother was just plain hideous!'

We should mourn
The astronomical
And almost comical
Growth of corn
In motion pictures
With strictures.
When clothes are shorn
A star is porn.

The strip show was slow in coming off, but fortunately there was no redress.

Morass: what the censors think the girls in films are showing these days.

Moron: what the censors think the girls in films should have.

The problem with short skirts is the upcreep.

These days, it's getting so that a diving-board is the only thing on which you can depend.

The Royal Navy used to insist on short haircuts for all the tars. They liked the crews to be shipshape and bristle fashion.

There is a place for humorists in the business world. Many a struggling company could use a fun raiser.

If you think there's a potential rapist hiding in the bushes, you should just cull the copse.

When he got home from the auction, he opened the writing desk and ten people fell out of it. Apparently, it was a missing persons' bureau.

They call a sensational report a canard because one canardly believe it.

To read dramatically, you should put more distress in one place than another.

Once upon a time, the king of a jungle tribe was given a golden throne by his affectionate people. The king was very proud of the throne, but very frightened of it being stolen. So, every night before he went to bed, he would hide the throne up on the rafters of his grass hut. Unfortunately, the rafters began to weaken and one night the rafter poles broke, the throne fell down, and the king was killed. As the tribe's witch doctor observed later, 'People who live in grass houses shouldn't stow thrones.'

A G.I. returned from Germany with an antique beer mug. To keep it safe, he put it in a special recess in his grandfather's clock. As the G.I. and his grandfather both lived in California, it was only a matter of time before an earthquake happened, and when it did, the clock was destroyed. But, amazingly, the beer mug hidden in the clock was safe. Which only goes to prove that a niche in time saves stein.

A West Country textile factory lost a considerable amount of its stock during a recent flood. The reason: too many brooks spoil the cloth.

Why was the librarian sad?
Because the books were in tiers!

Is tasteless extravagance for twenty-four hours a day baroque around the clock?

Crosswords are infuriating. They're always putting 1 across, which tends to get 1 down.

All music has a message; many a lyre has told the truth.

Perhaps it would be more truthful if today's newscasters were to begin, 'And here is a grief news report . . .'

I asked the hippie if the long hair was really his or whether he was just travelling under an assumed mane.

There was once a Peruvian prince who fished a maiden out of an enchanted lake. He married her before the Inca was dry!

'Has your film come back from the chemist's yet, Martha?'
'No, but someday my prints will come!'

The system of decimal notation has its points, but fractions are often vulgar.

Lecturer's comment scrawled at the foot of an essay written by one of his students: Thesis awful!

Is the dialogue of a horror film weird of mouth?

Sticks float, but then, they wood.

Most of today's best-selling paperbacks come from the trite side of the racks!

Misprint (presumably) seen in a newspaper classified ads section: 'Small apartment for runt.'

What with inflation, the price of haircuts is becoming shear nonsense.

Little ear of corn: 'Mummy, where did I come from?'
Mummy ear of corn: 'Well, dear, the stalk brought you.'

After the murder weapon had been found, the police began to search for the rifle owner.

'What did the man say when they told him that he'd just become the father of triplets?' 'I can't believe my census!'

There is an annual celebration on November 5th for homo-sexuals and lesbians. It's called Gay Folks Day.

'Going up! What floor, sir?'
'Elevate!'

'That makes 144,' he said grossly.

'Take my picture,' she snapped.

'I swallowed a lot of hay,' he said balefully.

'You might try looking in the attic,' she said loftily.

'You've used my bubble bath,' she foamed.

'I tripped,' he said lamely.

'That's a good yolk,' he cracked.

'We must rush this to the printers now,' he pressed.

'Turn on the radio,' he said with a short wave.

'That furnace is giving us trouble again,' he fumed.

'I fixed the loo,' he said, flushing.

'Give it to me on the level,' he said flatly.

'Don't needle me,' he said pointedly.

'Turn down that thermostat,' he said heatedly.

'Turn off the fridge,' he said icily.

'Drop the gun!' he said disarmingly.
'Never!' he shot back.

'We've struck oil,' he gushed.

'Was that the doorbell?' he chimed in.

'I just love onions!' he cried.

Perhaps the bore who constantly repeats the same joke has a one-crack mind?

16

THE PUN IS HERE TO SLAY

Puns can be made on all manner of subjects, as we have seen throughout this book. No exception to this rule are puns themselves.

A day without puns is like a day without sunshine; there is gloom for improvement.

The pun is the lowest form of humus – earthy.

Never point a pun at a friend, it might be loaded.

Punning was fecund nature to Shakespeare.

'She has made her fair share of puns, but I wouldn't want to quota.'

Old puns are like old shoes – they are hard on the soul.

If no pun is intended, then no punishment.

Every time Sherlock Holmes or Oliver Wendell Holmes cracked a pun, was it Holmes' pun?

'Pun my word' is the punster's favourite exclamation of surprise.

Pungent: what the author of this book is!

Punjab: a biting play on words, or repartee of the highest order.

Punnet: what the author of this book did when given a punnable subject.

Punsmith: a maker of puns.

Just remember: no matter how bad these puns may be, they could be verse!

And finally . . .
Pun friends: readers of this book.

NON-FICTION

GENERAL
☐ Guide to the Channel Islands — J. Anderson & E. Swinglehurst — 90p
☐ The Complete Traveller — Joan Bakewell — £1.95
☐ Time Out London Shopping Guide — Lindsey Bareham — £1.50
☐ World War 3 — Edited by Shelford Bidwell — £1.25
☐ Black Angels — Rupert Butler — £1.00
☐ Hand of Steel — Rupert Butler — £1.35
☐ A Walk Around the Lakes — Hunter Davies — £1.50
☐ Truly Murderous — John Dunning — 95p
☐ In Praise of Younger Men — Sandy Fawkes — 85p
☐ Wing Leader — Johnnie Johnson — £1.25
☐ Our Future: Dr. Magnus Pyke Predicts — — 95p
☐ Barbara Windsor's Book of Boobs — Barbara Windsor — £1.50

BIOGRAPHY/AUTOBIOGRAPHY
☐ Go-Boy — Roger Caron — £1.25
☐ George Stephenson — Hunter Davies — £1.50
☐ The Queen's Children — Donald Edgar — £1.25
☐ All of Me — Rose Neighbour — £1.00
☐ Tell Me Who I Am Before I Die — C. Peters with T. Schwarz — £1.00
☐ Boney M — J. Shearlaw and D. Brown — 90p
☐ Kiss — John Swenson — 90p

HEALTH/SELF-HELP/POCKET HEALTH GUIDES
☐ Pulling Your Own Strings — Dr. Wayne W. Dyer — 95p
☐ Woman X Two — Mary Kenny — 90p
☐ Cystitis: A Complete Self-help Guide — Angela Kilmartin — £1.00
☐ The Stress Factor — Donald Norfolk — 90p
☐ Fat is a Feminist Issue — Susie Orbach — 85p
☐ Related to Sex — Claire Rayner — £1.25
☐ The Working Women's Body Book — L. Rowen with B. Winkler — 95p
☐ Allergies — Robert Eagle — 65p
☐ Arthritis and Rheumatism — Dr. Luke Fernandes — 65p
☐ Back Pain — Dr. Paul Dudley — 65p
☐ Pre-Menstrual Tension — June Clark — 65p
☐ Migraine — Dr. Finlay Campbell — 65p
☐ Skin Trouble — Deanna Wilson — 65p

REFERENCE
☐ What's Wrong with your Pet? — Hugo Kerr — 95p
☐ Caring for Cats and Kittens — John Montgomery — 95p
☐ The Oscar Movies from A-Z — Roy Pickard — £1.25
☐ Questions of Law — Bill Thomas — 95p
☐ The Hamlyn Book of Amazing Information — — 80p
☐ The Hamlyn Family Medical Dictionary — — £2.50

GAMES & PASTIMES
☐ The Hamlyn Book of Brainteasers and Mindbenders — Ben Hamilton — 85p
☐ The Hamlyn Book of Crosswords Books 1, 2, 3, and 4 — — 60p
☐ The Hamlyn Book of Crosswords 5 — — 70p
☐ The Hamlyn Book of Wordways 1 — — 75p
☐ The Hamlyn Family Quiz Book — — 85p

NAME...

ADDRESS..

....

Write to Hamlyn Paperbacks Cash Sales, PO Box 11, Falmouth, Cornwall TR10 9EN.
Please indicate order and enclose remittance to the value of the cover price plus:
U.K.: 30p for the first book, 15p for the second book and 12p for each additional book ordered to a maximum charge of £1.29.
B.F.P.O. & EIRE: 30p for the first book, 15p for the second book plus 12p per copy for the next 7 books, thereafter 6p per book.
OVERSEAS: 50p for the first book plus 15p per copy for each additional book.
Whilst every effort is made to keep prices low it is sometimes necessary to increase cover prices and also postage and packing rates at short notice. Hamlyn Paperbacks reserve the right to show new retail prices on covers which may differ from those previously advertised in the text or elsewhere.